Remembering Adelia

Quilts Inspired by Her Diary

Kathleen Tracy

Martingale®
& COMPANY

Mission Statement

Dedicated to providing quality products and service to inspire creativity.

Credits

President & CEO: Tom Wierzbicki

Editor in Chief: Mary V. Green

Managing Editor: Tina Cook

Developmental Editor: Karen Costello Soltys

Technical Editor: Ursula Reikes

Copy Editor: Sheila Chapman Ryan

Design Director: Stan Green

Production Manager: Regina Girard

Illustrator: Laurel Strand

Cover & Text Designer: Regina Girard

Photographer: Brent Kane

Photo credits

The sources for the photographs in this book are listed below.

Des Plaines, Illinois, History Center: pages 6, 8, 9, 11, 27, 29, 43, 45, 56, 58, 59, and 72

McHenry County, Illinois, Historical Society: page 28

Evan Tracy: Photos of Adelia's diary and letters, pages 2 and 6

Remembering Adelia:
Quilts Inspired by Her Diary
© 2009 by Kathleen Tracy

That Patchwork Place® is an imprint of Martingale & Company®.

Martingale & Company
20205 144th Ave. NE
Woodinville, WA 98072-8478 USA
www.martingale-pub.com

Printed in China
14 13 12 11 10 09   8 7 6 5 4 3

Library of Congress Cataloging-in-Publication Data
Library of Congress Control Number: 2008050001

ISBN: 978-1-56477-865-9

For my mother

Acknowledgments

I am extremely grateful to all the people at Martingale & Company for making a book like this come to life.

Special thanks to Shari Caine, Archives Manager of the Des Plaines, Illinois, History Center, for permission to print excerpts from Adelia's diary and for her help with the background information and photos.

Many thanks to Nancy Fike and Grace Moline of the McHenry County Historical Society in Union, Illinois, for their help with research and photos.

Thanks to Cathy Reitan for piecing and appliquéing the blocks in the "Peony Star Quilt" on page 30.

Thanks to Dawn Larsen for her machine-quilting expertise seen in the following quilts: "Scrappy Star Quilt" (page 12), "Peony Star Quilt" (page 30), "Pink and Green Nine Patch Quilt" (page 34), "Orange Peel Quilt" (page 46), and "Calico Comfort Nine Patch Quilt" (page 60).

Thanks to my family and friends for their continued support of and pride in my creative pursuits. Mary Jane, I'm grateful for your friendship.

A special thank-you to all the fans of my first two books who encouraged me to keep going and write another one!

Contents

Adelia and her husband, Chester Bennett, 1865

Adelia's diary from 1861

Envelope adorned with Chester Bennett's writing and music, addressed to Adelia

Letter to Adelia from Chester before they were married

Introduction

While I was visiting local historical societies and researching pioneer families for my book *Prairie Children and Their Quilts* (Martingale & Company, 2006), I came across a small, leather-bound journal dated 1861. The journal was written by Adelia Thomas, a young woman of 19 who lived in a farming community in northern Illinois, miles away from the conflict when the Civil War began in the spring of that year.

Despite the intensity of the war, Adelia's journal focuses on family life and daily experiences and is filled with records of births, deaths, marriages, and social visits, like many other diaries written by young women during the nineteenth century. It's a wonderful look at what kinds of activities and thoughts occupied the lives and minds of young women at the beginning of that crucial time in America's history. Journal accounts like hers show us just how much sewing and quilting was a part of life for the average woman, and perhaps provided sustenance in times of strife, as well as fulfilling a desire to "do something" patriotic to help the soldiers. For many, quilting was also a way to preserve their memories.

The diary begins in January 1861, just months after President Lincoln was elected and before his inauguration in March. Fort Sumter was attacked by the Confederacy in April and Lincoln's first call for volunteer troops occurred a few days later. Most people, including Lincoln himself, expected that the war would be short-lived and over within a few months at the most, with minimal casualties. The actual loss of life that did occur (over 620,000) would have been unimaginable. As the year unfolds, we watch the crisis build as Adelia's friends, family, and neighbors join the fight to save the Union, some never to return.

Many quilts were made during this time in history, but few survived because of the devastation brought by the war. The quilts that did survive are excellent examples of quilting trends of the time. Inspired by a variety of antique quilts and the diary entries, the quilts and projects included in *Remembering Adelia* reflect some of these trends. The book includes 14 patterns for quilts and projects using traditional blocks in a variety of sizes. I've included doll-sized quilts because they're a great way to start quilting if you're a beginner and wall-sized quilts to make an easy transition to larger quilts.

I can't look at antique quilts without imagining the lives of the women who made them. Adelia's diary shows what daily life was really like for many women in the latter half of the nineteenth century. I hope this book will take quilters into that world. At first it may appear far removed from our own lives, but a closer glance will show that we are not so different from women who lived and quilted a century and a half ago. In remembering Adelia, I have tried to honor quiltmakers from the past and their extraordinary quilts that have been left to us as inspiration to re-create and treasure.

Winter 1861

Adelia Thomas Bennett, 1896

Adelia Thomas was born on July 29, 1842, in Pomfret, Vermont. Her family moved westward and settled in Cary Station, Illinois, circa 1843. According to the 1860 U.S. census, those living in the Thomas household included:

Name	Age
Elias Thomas	45
Hester Thomas	40
Adelia Thomas	17
Emma Thomas	15
Elias Thomas	12
Clara Thomas	8
Hester (Hettie) Thomas	5
Myron Harris	23
Frank Patterson	19

Myron and Frank were probably hired hands. James Thurston, mentioned frequently in the 1861 diary, was a family member from the East Coast who at the time was living with the Thomas family, as well as "Aunty," who arrived early in the year for an extended visit. Anna, also mentioned, seems to have been a woman hired to help with the housework. Other names mentioned frequently are: Mr. Smith (L., or Lester), a man Adelia corresponded with and possibly a suitor, who later enlisted in the 8th Illinois Cavalry, and Mr. Bennett, who eventually became Adelia's husband in 1865.

The photos used here of Adelia and her children were taken 20 to 30 years after her diary was written. Author's notes are enclosed in [brackets] in the diary entries.

January 15

It rained quite hard. Fair prospect of losing all the sleighing. Emma, James, and I did a large washing. Washed the kitchen floor. Mrs. Bennett called to get some milk for Mrs. Alcott. Went to singing school. The whole scrap of us had a good time coming home in the rain. Monroe Shales [is] twenty-one years old today and the suppositions are that he is to be married to Adeline Moore but that is false.

January 16

Charley Patterson came here. Myron, James, and him played "Euchre" several hours. Made a lot of mince pies. Went to singing school in the evening. Very crowded. After singing was over, Mr. Bennett sang "The Laziest Man in All the Town." A first-rate good song and sung very well too.

January 17

Did a little of everything and not much either. Sewed most of the day on mother's Zouave jacket [a common jacket style of the era, worn originally as a show of patriotism, named after the Zouave militia group] she had cut in Marengo. Father Howard preached at the schoolhouse, came here, and stayed all night. James and Myron went to Crystal Lake for that protracted meeting that has been held there for two weeks when folks lose their strength, scream and yell, and do all sorts of wicked things [a traveling revival meeting, probably].

January 26

Went to spelling school . . . then went to take a sleigh ride after. Maria and I did not want to go. The rest acted like fools.

January 29

Emma went to Woodstock with Frank Patterson and Mrs. Town. So very cold that they could not come home. But Emma, Carrie Griffith, Frank, and Sellers could go to McHenry and be gone till two o'clock at night.

The wind blew very cold all day. In the evening went to singing school. Came home freezing my ears.

January 31

Myron went to the station, brought home a paper with William's marriage in it. In the evening John Shaver, Lydia, Marg, Myron, and James went to Lorenzo Weaver's. They wanted I should go but I did not. Ironed until eleven o'clock at night. Went to bed pretty tired.

February 1

Worked nearly all day doing housework and did not accomplish much either. In the evening Father, Mother, Elias, Clara, and myself went and spent the evening at Melvira's. Had a great time playing "Euchre." James and I had a seat by the cupboard where we ate fried cakes and pickles.

Wash day

February 5

Worked all day nearly, cooking and washing dishes.

February 6

Mr. Bennett came here in the morning. We played the violin and melodeon [accordion] together several hours without stopping.

February 7

Mr. Bennett went home. Cold enough to freeze anybody. [I] worked like a streak all day and went to Mrs. Miller's to spend the evening. Stayed all night.

February 8

Still very cold but moderate towards noon so that it was quite comfortable. In the evening just as we were going to bed, a whole sleigh load of little folks came from Woodstock. Brought a dulcimer with them and danced on the carpet — staid until nearly two o'clock in the morning.

February 9

The company last night ate up all the victuals we had cooked in the house and this morning we had to go cooking again to be prepared in case we should have some more company. In the evening Mr. Sellers and Frank came and stayed all night.

February 10

Mr. Sellers carried Emma and Josephine [by carriage] to meeting at the schoolhouse then came back and got Mother and Frank. Emma and Josephine dressed alike. J. wore my jockey [hat] and cloak and delaine dress like Emma's. Rained like fun before they came back. Jo and Sellers went home in the afternoon. Went up into Aunty's room [in] the evening and had a circle [this may have been a prayer circle].

February 14

This morning it snowed and the wind blew very hard. Towards noon the weather moderated and then it rained. In the evening went to Mr. Sharp's spelling school and when we came home it snowed very hard. Mary Lincoln was there and made herself very conspicuous I thought. Maria Shaver spelled the school down. Valentine's day — never got one! Good.

February 20

Mr. Bennett came about noon. Sang and played together some. Called on William on our way to singing school. Bennett was playing just as the school commenced when he accidentally tipped over a fluid lamp, which created quite an excitement. Came near having a fight after school because Myron and some others were forbidden to play cards in singing school.

February 26

Mrs. Bennett came and spent the day. Did a lot of stitching for her on the machine. It took just one hour and a half. She sewed on my dress for me. Went to singing school in the evening.

March 5

Did the work and went to singing school in the evening. Charley called — brought a paper containing the President's inaugural address.

March 8

Snowed a little this morning but pleasant this afternoon. In the evening Father, Emma, and myself went to the station and joined the Sons of Temperance [a group that supported temperance and was a precursor to the Women's Christian Temperance movement; President Lincoln was a member]. The Wilcox girls and Hamilton girls were initiated at the same time.

March 10

Mr. Butler's baby buried today. Mother, Emma, and Elias went to the funeral. Mother stopped at Mr. Armstrong's to help them take care of their two children that are very sick.

March 11

Mother still at Mr. Armstrong's. Emma and I washed then went to Lyceum to hear Woman's [sic] Rights discussed. Pleased me to see the styles.

March 13

Got a letter from Lester [Smith].

March 26

Rained all day steady. Washed and cut carpet rags.

Kaufman-Bielefeldt farm. This is a farm in Des Plaines, Illinois, near the house Adelia and Chester lived in toward the latter part of the 1800s.

Scrappy Star Quilt

These scrappy blocks resemble the LeMoyne Star blocks that were popular during the nineteenth century. Those blocks were typically hand pieced using a template and set-in seams, but this easy version uses half-square triangles and is a simple way to replicate the look of the traditional block.

MATERIALS

Yardages are based on 42"-wide 100%-cotton fabrics.

1½ yards of medium blue print for outer border

⅛ yard *each* of 9 different medium blue prints for star backgrounds

¾ yard *total* of assorted reproduction print scraps, at least 4" x 4", for star points (you'll need 1 square for each star point)

¼ yard of red print for inner border

½ yard of gold print for binding

3¼ yards of backing fabric

58" x 58" piece of cotton batting

CUTTING

From *each* of the medium blue prints for star backgrounds, cut:

◆ 4 squares, 3½" x 3½" (36 total)

◆ 4 squares, 3⅞" x 3⅞"; cut each square once diagonally to yield 8 half-square triangles (72 total)

From the reproduction print scraps for star points, cut:

◆ 72 squares, 3⅞" x 3⅞"; cut each square once diagonally to yield 2 half-square triangles (144 total)

From the red print, cut:

◆ 4 strips, 1¾" x 42"

From the medium blue print, cut on the *lengthwise* grain:

◆ 4 strips, 6" x 52"

From the gold print, cut:

◆ 5 strips, 2½" x 42"

MAKING THE BLOCKS

The best way to put this quilt together is to make one block at a time using a variety of fabric scraps. Some prints may be used more than once. For each block, choose one medium blue print for the star background and eight different reproduction prints for the star points. Arrange the pieces to form a block. I always cut more scrap squares than I need and play with the different reproduction prints until I like the arrangement of the pieces. Don't be afraid to place unusual colors next to each other. Just be sure to add a bit of contrast so that the stars don't blend into the background.

1. Sew a reproduction print half-square triangle to a medium blue half-square triangle. Press. Make eight for each block.

Make 8
for each block.

2. Sew the remaining reproduction print half-square triangles together in pairs, putting the fabrics next to each other as you want them placed in the block. Press. Make four for each block.

Make 4
for each block.

3. To make the blocks, sew the medium blue squares and the half-square-triangle units together into four rows as shown. Be sure to use matching reproduction prints in each star point. Press the seam allowances in the opposite direction from row to row. Sew the rows together and press the seam allowances in one direction. Make nine blocks.

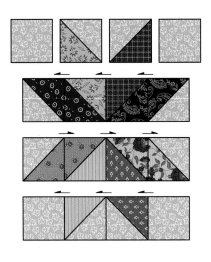

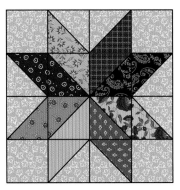

Make 9.

ASSEMBLING THE QUILT TOP

1. Lay out the blocks in three rows of three blocks each. Sew the blocks together into rows and press the seam allowances in opposite directions from row to row. Sew the rows together and press the seam allowances in one direction.

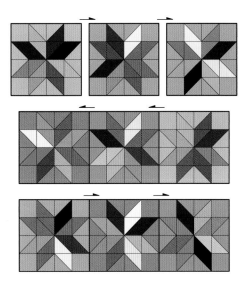

2. Measure the length of the quilt through the center. Cut two of the 1¾" x 42" red strips to fit and sew them to the sides of the quilt top. Press the seam allowance toward the border. Measure the width of the quilt through the center, including the side borders just added. Cut the remaining two 1¾" x 42" red strips to fit and sew them to the top and bottom of the quilt top. Press toward the border.

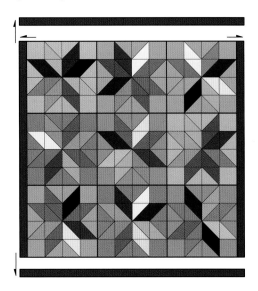

3. Measure the length of the quilt through the center. Cut two of the 6" x 52" blue strips to fit and sew them to the sides of the quilt top. Press the seam allowances toward the outer border. Measure the width of the quilt through the center, including the side borders just added. Cut the remaining two 6" x 52" blue strips to fit and sew them to the top and bottom of the quilt top. Press toward the outer border.

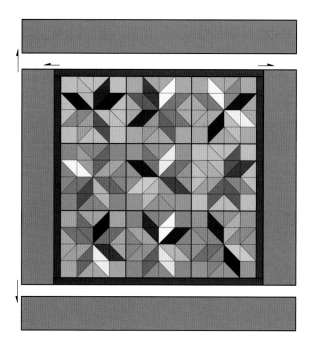

FINISHING THE QUILT

1. Layer the quilt top, batting, and backing; baste the layers together as shown in "Putting the Quilt Together" on page 77.

2. This quilt was machine quilted with an overall Baptist Fan pattern, a popular quilting design of the nineteenth century.

3. Attach the binding to the quilt, referring to "Binding" on page 78.

4. See "Adding a Label" on page 79.

Keeping It Simple

More often than not, antique quilts were scrap quilts. One of the distinctive things about scrap quilts is that they contain many different pieces of fabric and frequently have a busy look. In making your quilts, try to keep the busyness to a minimum by using a certain favorite color (or two) and repeating it throughout. Include some contrast by placing light shades next to medium or dark shades so that the design is obvious and the fabrics don't just blend into one another. You may also wish to use a simple block or design. Keeping the design simple lets certain fabrics stand out more, and prevents the eye from wandering. A great scrap quilt encourages the eye to focus on the pattern and fabrics and doesn't allow the viewer to become bored or frustrated with the design.

Some quilters like to place their fabrics in a completely random fashion when making a scrap quilt, but I prefer to take time to play with and arrange my fabrics until I find a pleasing color scheme and pattern that makes good use of contrast. Use small amounts of colors you wouldn't usually think go together. Colors like poison green, purple, double pink, and black can give a "kick" to a scrap quilt and were often used in quilts from the past. Also, pay close attention to value, and don't make the mistake of using too many medium-toned prints within a block. Place a vivid print next to one that is quieter, and let a favorite fabric "speak" by placing it next to a more muted print for an interesting, antique-inspired quilt.

Lincoln's Platform Quilt

Abraham Lincoln was elected president in November 1860 and inaugurated in March 1861. The name of the Lincoln's Platform quilt block was inspired by his position on slavery.

MATERIALS

Yardages are based on 42"-wide 100%-cotton fabrics.

½ yard of beige floral print for outer border

¼ yard of light blue print for setting squares

⅛ yard of black-and-blue print for inner border

⅛ yard of medium blue print for inner border

Scraps of 3 blue prints (or three fat quarters) for blocks

Scraps of 2 red prints (or two fat quarters) for blocks

Scraps of a butternut gold print (or one fat eighth) for center block

¼ yard of indigo print for binding

1 yard of backing fabric

28" x 28" piece of cotton batting

CUTTING

From *each of 2* of the blue print scraps or fat quarters, cut:
+ 4 squares, 2⅜" x 2⅜" (8 total)
+ 8 rectangles, 1¼" x 2" (16 total)
+ 24 squares, 1¼" x 1¼" (48 total)

From the remaining blue print scrap or fat quarter, cut:
+ 2 squares, 2⅜" x 2⅜"
+ 13 squares, 1¼" x 1¼"

From *each* of the 2 red prints, cut:
+ 4 squares, 2⅜" x 2⅜" (8 total)
+ 26 squares, 1¼" x 1¼" (52 total)

From the butternut gold print, cut:
+ 2 squares, 2⅜" x 2⅜"
+ 4 rectangles, 1¼" x 2"
+ 12 squares, 1¼" x 1¼"

From the light blue print, cut:
+ 4 squares, 5¾" x 5¾"

From the black-and-blue print, cut:
+ 2 strips, 1¼" x 16¼"

From the medium blue print, cut:
+ 2 strips, 1¼" x 17¾"

From the beige floral print, cut:
+ 2 strips, 4" x 17¾"
+ 2 strips, 4" x 24¾"

From the indigo print, cut:
+ 3 strips, 2½" x 42"

MAKING THE BLOCKS

There are four blue-and-red Lincoln's Platform blocks; two are made from one set of blue and red prints and two are made from a different set of blue and red prints. The block in the center is made from a butternut gold print and a medium blue print. Select the fabrics for each block before you begin in order to simplify piecing the blocks.

1. Draw a diagonal line from corner to corner on the wrong side of each 2⅜" blue square. Layer a marked blue square on top of each 2⅜" red square, right sides together. Layer the remaining 2⅜" blue squares with the 2⅜" butternut squares. Stitch ¼" from the line on both sides. Cut on the drawn line. Press the seam allowances toward the darker fabric. Make 16 red/blue half-square-triangle units and 4 butternut/blue half-square-triangle units.

Make 16.   Make 4.

2. Sew matching red/blue half-square-triangle units together with one matching blue 1¼" x 2" rectangle to make the top and bottom rows of the block. Press the seam allowances toward the rectangle. Sew two matching 1¼" x 2" blue rectangles and a matching 1¼" red print square together to make the middle row. Press toward the rectangles. Sew the rows together. Press. Make four red/blue blocks. Repeat with butternut and blue pieces to make one block.

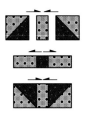

Make 4.   Make 1.

3. Using matching prints for each block, sew two 1¼" blue print squares together with three 1¼" red print squares to make side units for each block. Press the seam allowances toward the darker fabric. Sew these units to the sides of a block. Sew four 1¼" blue print squares together with three 1¼" red print squares to make top and bottom units for each block. Press toward the darker fabric. Sew these to the top and bottom. Sew 1¼" butternut and 1¼" blue squares together in the same manner for the butternut/blue block.

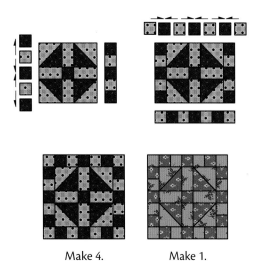

Make 4.   Make 1.

ASSEMBLING THE QUILT TOP

1. Lay out the blocks and setting squares as shown. Sew the blocks and squares into rows. Press the seam allowances toward the setting squares. Sew the rows together. Press.

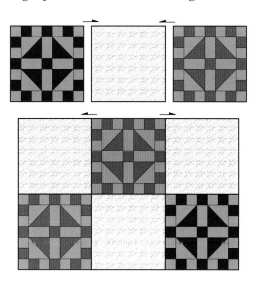

2. Sew the black-and-blue 1¼" x 16¼" strips to the top and bottom of the quilt top. Press the seam allowances toward the border. Sew the medium blue 1¼" x 17¾" strips to the sides of the quilt top. Press toward the border.

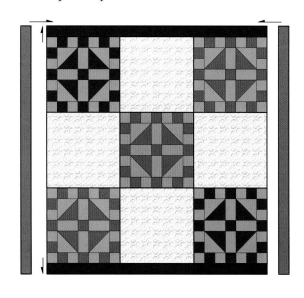

3. Sew the 4" x 17¾" beige floral strips to the sides of the quilt top, pressing the seam allowances toward the outer border. Sew the two 4" x 24¾" beige floral strips to the top and bottom of the quilt top. Press toward the outer border.

FINISHING THE QUILT

1. Layer the quilt top, batting, and backing; baste the layers together as shown in "Putting the Quilt Together" on page 77.

2. Quilt a flower design in the plain blue blocks and in the ditch along the inner border. Quilt an X in the Lincoln's Platform blocks. Using a bowl, trace a scallop design with a quilt marking pencil in the outer border; then quilt the scallops.

3. Attach the binding to the quilt, referring to "Binding" on page 78.

4. See "Adding a Label" on page 79.

Organizing Your Scraps

The Civil War drained the nation's economy and quilts made during that era used scraps or snippets of worn clothing since new fabrics were often hard to come by. Many of the blocks in the quilts in this book were made from scraps from my scrap basket, just as the women of the nineteenth century utilized what they had left over or were able to salvage.

If you like antique quilts and love to reproduce that old-fashioned look, then you probably have an assortment of scraps useful for making your own scrappy quilts. I used to keep my scraps in baskets and when a basket became full of strips or small leftover squares, the solution would be to just add another basket and then another to contain them. I now organize even my smallest scraps by color in clear plastic bags that are stored in a bin on a shelf in my sewing space. This system works well for me. When I am working on a scrappy quilt, I place the bin with colorful bags nearby to simplify the process of choosing my scraps for the blocks.

Tumbling Blocks Quilt

This little Tumbling Blocks quilt was inspired by a photo in a magazine of a larger Tumbling Blocks quilt made in 1882 by President Calvin Coolidge when he was a child. I pieced it by hand, in the same way that a similar quilt may have been pieced in the nineteenth century, which allowed for more control and accuracy than if pieced entirely by machine. If you've never hand pieced before, try it in this project—you may be surprised to find out how much fun it is.

MATERIALS

Yardages are based on 42"-wide 100%-cotton fabrics.

⅛ yard of brown reproduction print for border

⅛ yard of tan reproduction print for border

Scraps of assorted prints in light, medium, and
  dark shades, each at least 2½" x 5", for 168
  diamonds

¼ yard of indigo print for binding

⅞ yard of backing fabric

20" x 30" piece of cotton batting

Template plastic

CUTTING

From the brown reproduction print, cut:
◆ 2 strips, 1¾" x 24⅛"

From the tan reproduction print, cut:
◆ 2 strips, 2¼" x 19½"

From the indigo print, cut:
◆ 2 strips, 2" x 42"

MAKING THE BLOCKS

1. Using the pattern on page 22, trace the
   diamond shape onto template plastic and
   cut it out on the line. Using a water-soluble
   marking pen, trace around the template on
   the right side of the assorted scraps. Cut
   out each shape, leaving a scant ¼" seam
   allowance all around. Cut 168.

2. On the wrong side of each diamond, place a
   small dot where the seams will intersect. Use
   an accurate ¼" seam allowance.

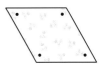

3. For accurate piecing, you will need to sew a
   Y seam. With right sides together, sew a light
   print diamond to a medium print diamond,
   sewing from dot to dot and avoiding
   stitching into the ¼" seam allowances. Sew
   a dark print diamond to one edge of the
   Y-shaped sewn unit in the same way. Stitch
   the other edge of the dark print diamond to
   the finished unit. Make 54 blocks (you will
   have six diamonds left over; set these aside
   for later).

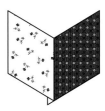
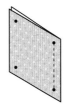

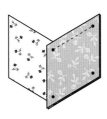

Make 54.

ASSEMBLING THE QUILT TOP

1. Lay out the hexagons in nine rows of six blocks each. Sew the hexagons together into rows. Sew six diamond pieces to the bottom edge of the quilt top to fill out the rows. Press.

2. Using a long ruler, trim the top and bottom edges of the quilt, leaving a ¼" seam allowance. Trim the side edges even with the edge of the shorter rows of blocks as shown.

3. Sew the 1¾" x 24⅛" brown strips to the sides of the quilt top. Press the seam allowances toward the border. Sew the 2¼" x 19½" tan strips to the top and bottom of the quilt top. Press toward the border.

FINISHING THE QUILT

1. Layer the quilt top, batting, and backing; baste the layers together as shown in "Putting the Quilt Together" on page 77.

2. Quilt ¼" along the blocks in horizontal rows.

3. Attach the binding to the quilt, referring to "Binding" on page 78.

4. See "Adding a Label" on page 79.

Diamond
Cut 168.

*Pattern does not
include seam allowance.*

Fabric-Covered Journal

Create a journal to record your quilt projects and leave a legacy of
your own. Imagine how fortunate we'd be if all quilters from the past
had signed and dated their quilts or left a record of their projects.

FINISHED BOOK COVER: 7¼" x 10¼"

The materials and cutting instructions below are for a journal that measures 3¾" x 6¾" closed, 7¼" x 10¼" opened flat. See sidebar on page 25 for making a different-sized journal.

MATERIALS

Yardages are based on 42"-wide 100%-cotton fabrics.

1 fat quarter of red print for journal lining

1 fat quarter of blue striped fabric for journal front and back

Tan print scrap, at least 4" x 9", for journal spine

9" x 14" piece of thin cotton batting

12"-long piece of green grosgrain ribbon, ⅜" wide

9"-long piece of lace trim, 1" wide

3¾" x 6¾" loose-leaf notebook with 6 rings (the one I used was made by Mead)

CUTTING

From the red print, cut:
✦ 1 rectangle, 8" x 14"

From the blue striped fabric, cut:
✦ 2 rectangles, 5¾" x 8"

From the tan print, cut:
✦ 1 rectangle, 3½" x 8"

From the batting, cut:
✦ 1 rectangle, 8" x 14"

ASSEMBLING THE JOURNAL COVER

1. To make the front and back cover of the journal, sew the two blue rectangles to each side of the tan print rectangle.

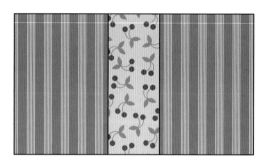

2. Lay the strip of ribbon down the center on the right side of the tan piece of the cover; pin in place at the center top. Turn the cover over and place it on top of the red print lining rectangle, so that the right sides are together. Place the batting on the bottom below the lining. Using a ¼" seam allowance, sew the layers together, leaving a 2" opening for turning. Be careful not to catch the free end of the ribbon in any seams.

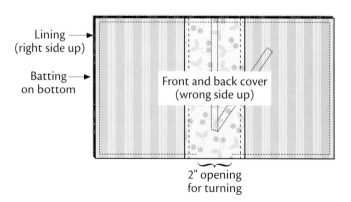

Lining (right side up)

Batting on bottom

Front and back cover (wrong side up)

2" opening for turning

3. Turn the cover right side out through the opening and press flat. Fold the seam allowances at the 2" opening to the inside,

press, and pin. Open the journal and place it on top of the inside cover. Fold the sides toward the opened journal and pin at the top and bottom of either side. Remove the journal and stitch ⅛" all around the edge with a neutral-colored thread. Do not stitch over the ribbon. Press.

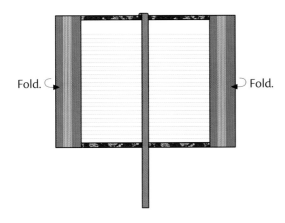

4. Pin the strip of lace on the front next to the tan print and stitch in place. Trim the edges of the lace even with the edges of the cover.

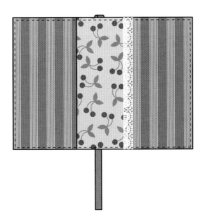

Adjust the Size

To make a cover for a different-sized journal, you'll need to make a paper template. Lay the journal open onto a piece of paper that is larger than the book (a brown paper bag cut open works fine). Add ½" at the top and bottom of the journal and 2" on either side. Draw the rectangle in pencil on the paper and cut out. Mark a 3½" segment in the center for the journal spine.

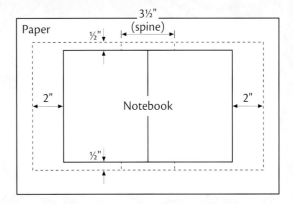

To cut the lining, lay the template on the red print and cut out. To cut the pieces for the front and back cover, cut a piece of fabric for the spine, which will be the same size as the center spine on the template. Then cut two pieces for the sides the same size as the larger side rectangles on the template, adding ¼" to the long side for a seam allowance.

Refer to steps 1–3 on page 24 to assemble the journal.

Spring 1861

April 1

Received an "April Fool" letter from Mr. Bennett.

April 3

Aunty went to Mrs. Shaver's in the afternoon. Mother, Emma, and I cut carpet rags all the afternoon.

April 4

Whitewashed and cleaned the buttery today. Mrs. Morley worked here today.

April 5

Cleaned the boys' chamber this forenoon. Made my arms lame from whitewashing. In the afternoon the two Lewis girls, Em Dodd, Mrs. Vosburgh, and Jule Harback were at our house. Em stayed all night.

April 6

Raining still this morning. After dinner it stopped a little so that Em and I went to William's. The Lewis girls and Jule were there. Stayed all night. Em helped me to make over one of mother's dresses for me in the forenoon. Cornelia Lewis dressed in the character of an old woman.

April 8

Washed this morning. Clara and I went to Woodstock in the afternoon. Edwin went to singing school with me in the evening. Nine years ago today since my little brother died.

April 12

Aunt Harriet came down to Edwin's and stayed to dinner. They were all busy sewing so I got the dinner. It rained all afternoon very hard.

The rebels commenced bombarding Fort Sumter. The first commencement of the war!

April 15

Went up to Aunt Harriet's in the forenoon. Helped her to fix Hattie and Willie for the concert this evening. Mr. Smith [L. or Lester] called there in the afternoon. Went to the concert with him. Went to Edwin's afterward. Got home before they did—found the door locked and had to wait until they came before I could get in. [April 15 was Lincoln's first call for volunteer troops.]

April 16

Tuesday Tyler came down to Edwin's in his motherly way to give me a little advice. Saw four carloads of soldiers pass by.

April 18

Mr. Smith called a little while.

April 19

Went and called to Carrie's. She went to the depot with me. Saw John Murphy, John Medlar, Mr. Smith, Frank Wait, Emma Church, and a good many others. Three carloads of soldiers passed by and their artillery with them.

April 26

Saw Matt Butler having his picture taken before going to the war.

April 28

Bent the Sabbath a little by making a flag to put up on our house. Went over to Bill's and Mr. Vosburgh's. He had taken pictures all day for the volunteers. Mother's forty-second birthday.

April 29

Fired several guns and cheered for our flag. Bid good-bye to Frank.

May 10

Made some pies in the morning and got things ready for Mother and Lydia Patterson who came on the morning train. Frank came to supper for the last time, for he left for Algonquin this afternoon. Mother bought some trimming for our silk dresses and Clara and Hettie some coral beads.

May 13

Could not wash today for we had no water so I worked on my bed quilt. Mrs. Harback called in the afternoon to invite us there to a quilting on Wednesday and to get some music for the quartet. They were appointed to sing in the Division next Friday. ["Quiltings," or sewing circles, were common as the war started and President Lincoln urged women to support the war effort by making bedding for the soldiers.]

May 14

Washed today. Mrs. Owen sent over word for more carpet rags immediately so we put right into them all of us. Henry Paddock's little boy buried today.

May 15

Cut rags all the forenoon as fast as we could. Went to the quilting in the afternoon. Received a piece of music from Mr. Bennett of his own composition — "Look on the Bright Side." William Robinson's baby buried today.

May 16

Ironed in the morning while Emma sowed flower seeds in the garden. Not much else done besides our usual work, which amounts to something.

May 20

Rained all night and filled the cistern up full. Washed and did most of the ironing.

Quilting circle

Civil War soldier from McHenry, Illinois

May 29

All went to the picnic except Anna, Aunty, and Myron. Had an excellent time and the day [was] very pleasant. Went round the square in a procession. Had a flag and martial music. Then to the river where we had dinner and enjoyed ourselves in any way that we chose. Emma and I went to Melvira's for dinner, then went to Pingry's to a dance. Several of the soldiers home from Freeport. Matt Butler home too.

May 30

Felt pretty well used up. Emma never got up until after eight o'clock. Cornelia came to invite Mother to William's for a quilting in the afternoon. I papered Mother's bedroom then she went away in the evening.

June 3

Juliette came home with me to make our new silk dresses. Marg Shaver's twentieth birthday. Stephen A. Douglas died in Chicago this morning.

June 8

Juliette came towards noon and Emma and I finished some dark-colored dresses for the little girls.

June 10

I washed all alone for Emma had a sore hand. Juliette came in the afternoon to work. Emma sat down and sewed with her and left me the work to do all alone. Myron [is] twenty-five years old today.

June 11

Today thought we would iron but it was so warm that we could not get up spunk enough to finish so in the afternoon sewed on the children's aprons. Finished Emma's silk dress. Real pretty.

June 12

This morning finished ironing. Mother would not let us go to Mrs. Shaver's for she had concluded to have a quilting the next day. Did some cooking in the afternoon and after supper went [on] horseback over to Mrs. Miller's to invite her. Had an excellent time and a good ride.

June 13

Washed the windows in the dining room and cleaned the piazza floor. Made two chicken pies then cleaned the dining room up. Mrs. Miller came to our quilting in the forenoon. Had a grand time. All the women in the neighborhood here and the girls too. Got the quilt all done then went home with Juliette to Mrs. Vosburgh's. Father and Clara went to Woodstock in the morning. Heard the drums clear from Wauconda when I was coming home from Vosburgh's.

June 14

Put on a comfortable at tack today. [This means she tied a comforter.]

June 15

Emma sick and Anna too. Finished tacking the comforter. Mrs. Welch helped clean the parlor and upstairs. The wind blew very hard indeed all day so it was not safe for folks that wear large hoops to be out. Charley Patterson at our house in the afternoon.

June 21

Father and Mother went to McHenry and took Cornelia with them. Bought some lace for a bertha [corset] for me and some calico for a dress. Cleaned the kitchen floor and made some pies. The boys went to John Goodwin's to help raise a barn.

June 22

Mr. Smith came in the afternoon.

May Jefferson, friend of Adelia's family, in kitchen

June 27

Mother, Emma, and I went to Mrs. Miller's to a quilting in the afternoon. I stayed all night to finish the quilt. Had a real good visit with the folks there and lots of fun.

June 28

Quilted all day from seven in the morning until five in the afternoon. Had a real good visit with Mrs. Miller. Received a letter from Anderson Murphy inviting us to Woodstock to a picnic at the close of school. Nina Hamilton said Myron told her I was to be married on the Fourth. News to me entirely. But one very important thing they left out. Who it was to!

June 29

Emma and I sewed most of the day.

Peony Star Quilt

Looking through a book on antique quilts from the nineteenth century
inspired me to make this quilt featuring an unusual version of the Peony
Star block. The colorful scraps used in this quilt are reminiscent of the
vivid colors in old-fashioned country gardens and the brown striped
reproduction print used in the border gives a subtle antique touch.

MATERIALS

Yardages are based on 42"-wide 100%-cotton fabrics.

1⅝ yards of brown striped print that runs lengthwise for borders

9 fat eighths of assorted neutral or shirting prints for block backgrounds

9 fat eighths of assorted medium prints for peonies

½ yard of light floral print for setting and corner triangles

⅜ yard of beige reproduction print for setting squares

Scraps of assorted green prints for stems and leaves (some prints may be repeated)

⅝ yard of pink print for binding

3¼ yards of fabric for backing

58" x 58" piece of cotton batting

Template plastic

CUTTING

From *each* of the fat eighths of assorted neutral or shirting prints, cut:
+ 3 squares, 3⅛" x 3⅛" (27 total)
+ 3 squares, 2¾" x 2¾" (27 total)
+ 1 square, 5" x 5" (9 total)

From *each* of the fat eighths of medium prints, cut:
+ 3 squares, 3⅛" x 3⅛" (27 total)
+ 3 squares, 2¾" x 2¾" (27 total)

From the scraps of assorted green prints for stems and leaves, cut:
+ 9 strips, 1¼" x 8½"

From the beige reproduction print, cut:
+ 4 squares, 9½" x 9½"

From the light floral print, cut:
+ 2 squares, 7¼" x 7¼"; cut each square once diagonally to yield 4 corner triangles
+ 2 squares, 14" x 14"; cut each square *twice* diagonally to yield 8 setting triangles

From the brown striped print, cut on the *lengthwise* grain:
+ 4 strips, 6¼" x 52"

From the pink print, cut:
+ 7 strips, 2½" x 42"

MAKING THE BLOCKS

For each Peony Star block, choose a medium print, a neutral background print, and green scraps for the stems and leaves.

1. Use a 1¼" x 8½" green scrap strip to make a stem, referring to "Making Stems and Handles" on page 76. Pin the finished stem diagonally on a 5" neutral or shirting print square.

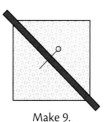

Make 9.

2. Using the pattern on page 33, trace the leaf onto template plastic and cut out on the line. Using a water-soluble marking pen, trace around the template on the right side of a green print scrap. Cut out the shape, leaving a scant ¼" seam allowance all around. Make two matching leaves for each block. Set aside.

3. Draw a diagonal line from corner to corner on the wrong side of a 3⅛" neutral or shirting print square. Layer the marked square on top of a 3⅛" medium print square, right sides together. Sew ¼" from the line on both sides. Cut on the drawn line and press. Make six for each block.

Make 6
for each block.

4. Sew a unit from step 3 together with a 2¾" matching neutral or shirting print square. Press. Make three for each block. Sew the remaining three units from step 3 together with matching 2¾" print squares. Press. Make three for each block.

Make 3
for each block.

Make 3
for each block.

5. Lay out the matching units from step 4 as shown, sew, and press. Make three for each block.

Make 3
for each block.

6. Sew matching units from step 5 together with the 5" square from step 1 into rows. Sew the rows together and press. Appliqué the stem and leaves to the block, referring to "Appliqué" on page 75. Make nine blocks.

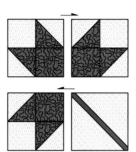 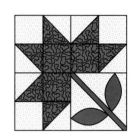

Make 9.

ASSEMBLING THE QUILT TOP

1. Lay out the blocks, the beige setting squares, and the light floral side and corner setting triangles in diagonal rows. Sew the blocks, setting squares, and side triangles into rows. Press the seam allowances toward the setting squares and side triangles.

2. Sew the rows together, matching seam intersections. Add the corner triangles and press toward the triangles. If necessary, trim and square up the quilt top, making sure to leave ¼" beyond the points of all the blocks for seam allowances.

3. Measure the length of the quilt top through the center. Cut two of the 6¼" x 52" brown strips to fit and sew them to the sides of the quilt top. Press the seam allowances toward the border. Measure the width of the quilt top through the center, including the borders just added. Cut the remaining 6¼" x 52" brown strips to fit and sew them to the top and bottom of the quilt top. Press toward the border.

FINISHING THE QUILT

1. Layer the quilt top, batting, and backing; baste the layers together as shown in "Putting the Quilt Together" on page 77.

2. This quilt was machine quilted with an allover stipple pattern.

3. Attach the binding to the quilt, referring to "Binding" on page 78.

4. See "Adding a Label" on page 79.

Leaf
Cut 18.

Pattern does not include seam allowance.

Pink and Green Nine Patch Quilt

While we often think of quilts from the Civil War era as being made from darker shades of fabrics, pink and green prints were actually quite popular during the time period.

MATERIALS

Yardages are based on 42"-wide 100%-cotton fabrics.

2 yards of pink print for borders

¾ yard of indigo print for sashing and corner blocks

¼ yard *total* of assorted pink print scraps for block centers

¼ yard *total* of assorted pink scraps for cornerstones

20 strips, each 2¾" x 20", of assorted green prints for blocks (some prints may be repeated)

20 assorted sets of 4 matching pink print squares, each 2¾" x 2¾", for block corners (80 squares total; some prints may be repeated)

½ yard of green print for binding

3½ yards of fabric for backing

63" x 74" piece of cotton batting

CUTTING

From *each* of the 20 green print strips, cut:
✦ 4 rectangles, 2¾" x 5" (80 total)

From the assorted scraps of pink prints for block centers, cut:
✦ 20 squares, 5" x 5"

From the indigo print, cut:
✦ 49 rectangles, 2¾" x 9½"
✦ 4 squares, 4½" x 4½"

From the assorted scraps of pink prints for cornerstones, cut:
✦ 30 squares, 2¾" x 2¾"

From the pink print for borders, cut from the *lengthwise* grain:
✦ 4 strips, 4½" x 62"

From the green print for binding, cut:
✦ 7 strips, 2½" x 42"

MAKING THE BLOCKS

For each Nine Patch block, lay out four matching 2¾" pink print squares, four matching 2¾" x 5" green print rectangles, and one contrasting 5" pink print square as shown. Sew the pieces into rows, pressing the seam allowances of the top and bottom rows toward the corner squares and the seam allowances of the middle row toward the center square. Sew the rows together and press toward the center. Make 20 blocks.

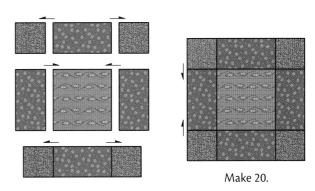

Make 20.

ASSEMBLING THE QUILT TOP

1. Sew four blocks together with five indigo sashing strips to make a row. Press the seam allowances toward the sashing strips. Make five rows.

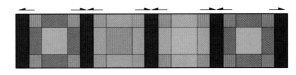

Make 5 rows.

2. Sew four sashing strips together with five 2¾" pink print squares to make a sashing row. Press the seam allowances toward the sashing strips. Make six rows.

Make 6 rows.

3. Sew the rows of blocks and sashing rows together, beginning and ending with a sashing row. Press the seam allowances toward the sashing rows.

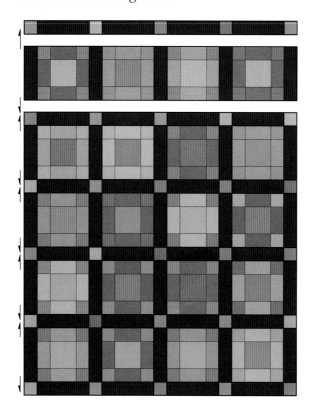

4. Measure the width of the quilt top through the center. Cut two of the 4½" x 62" pink print strips to fit the top and bottom of the quilt top. Measure the length of the quilt top through the center, and cut the remaining

4½" x 62" pink strips to fit the sides of the quilt top. Sew border strips to the top and bottom of the quilt top, and press the seam allowances toward the border. Sew a 4½" indigo print square to each end of the border strips for the sides and press toward the border. Sew these strips to the sides of the quilt top and press toward the border.

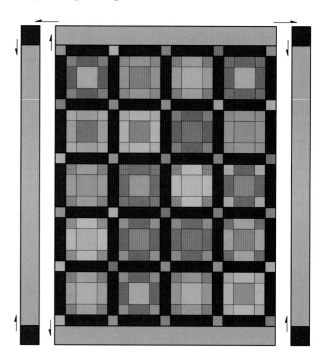

FINISHING THE QUILT

1. Layer the quilt top, batting, and backing; baste the layers together as shown in "Putting the Quilt Together" on page 77.

2. This quilt was machine quilted using a simple floral design.

3. Attach the binding to the quilt, referring to "Binding" on page 78.

4. See "Adding a Label" on page 79.

Flowerpot Appliqué Wall Quilt

Ruching, a French term meaning to gather or pleat, was popular in the nineteenth century. This little wall quilt with raw-edge ruffled flowers was inspired by photos of women's clothing that included ruching at the sleeves, necklines, and bodices. Lace was expensive during the war, and ruching made from fabric or ribbon may have been used as an alternative.

MATERIALS

Yardages are based on 42"-wide 100%-cotton fabrics.

¾ yard of blue-and-tan floral striped print that runs lengthwise for borders

Scraps of 6 assorted prints, each at least 2" x 10", for flowers

Scraps of 5 assorted green prints for leaves and stems

Scraps of 4 beige prints (2 the same), each at least 7" x 7", for appliqué background

Scrap of medium blue print, at least 7" x 7", for flowerpot

Scrap of tan print, at least 7" x 7", for base of flowerpot

¼ yard of brown print for binding

¾ yard of backing fabric

21" x 27" piece of cotton batting

Pinking shears

2 buttons, ⅝" in diameter, and 3 buttons, ¾" in diameter

Template plastic

CUTTING

From the medium blue print, cut:
✦ 1 square, 6⅞" x 6⅞"

From the tan print, cut:
✦ 1 square, 6⅞" x 6⅞"

From the beige prints, cut:
✦ 4 squares, 6½" x 6½"

From the assorted prints for flowers, cut:
✦ 1 strip, 1" x 9½" (double-flower center)
✦ 1 strip, 1½" x 9½" (double-flower outer piece)
✦ 2 strips, 1" x 6" (small flowers)
✦ 2 strips, 1¼" x 7" (medium flowers)

From the assorted green prints, cut *on the bias*:
✦ 1 strip, 1¼" x 9"
✦ 2 strips, 1¼" x 5"
✦ 2 strips, 1¼" x 5½"

From the blue-and-tan floral striped print, cut:
- 2 strips, 3¾" x 18½", from the *lengthwise* grain
- 2 strips, 3¾" x 19", from the *crosswise* grain

From the brown print, cut:
- 3 strips, 2½" x 42"

MAKING THE APPLIQUÉ BACKGROUND

1. Draw a diagonal line from corner to corner on the wrong side of the 6⅞" tan print square. Layer it with the 6⅞" medium blue square, right sides together. Stitch ¼" from the line on both sides and cut on the drawn line. Press the seam allowances toward the darker fabric. Sew the two half-square-triangle units together to make the flowerpot base. Press.

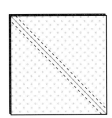 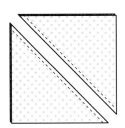

Make 2.

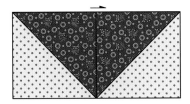

2. Sew the four 6½" beige print squares together to make a four-patch unit. Press.

3. Sew the flowerpot base to the four-patch unit, leaving a ½" space unsewn in the center to insert the stem of the appliqué later. Press the seam allowances toward the flowerpot base.

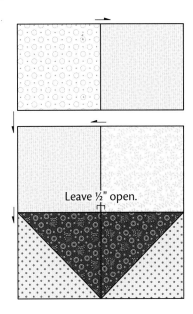

Leave ½" open.

MAKING THE FLOWERS, STEMS, AND LEAVES

1. Make two small and two medium flowers as follows. Trim one long edge of each 1" x 6" and 1¼" x 7" strip with pinking shears. Sew a line of basting stitches (by hand or machine) about ⅛" from the straight edge, leaving a 2" length of thread. Pull the thread to gather. Form the ruffled piece into

a circle and stitch the ends together to make the flower. Press flat.

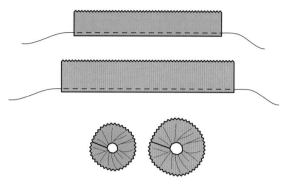

Make 2 small and 2 medium flowers.

2. Make one double flower as follows. Trim one long edge of each 1" x 9½" and 1½" x 9½" strip with pinking shears. Layer the strips with the narrow strip on top and straight edges aligned. Sew a line of basting stitches (by hand or machine) about ⅛" from the straight edge, leaving a 2" length of thread. Pull the thread to gather. Form the ruffled piece into a circle and stitch the ends together to make the flower. Press flat.

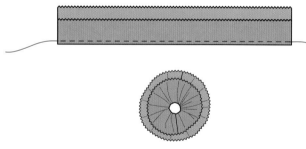

Make 1 double flower.

3. Referring to "Making Stems and Handles" on page 76 and using the green strips, make one stem from a 1¼" x 9" strip, make two stems from the 1¼" x 5" strips, and make two stems from the 1¼" x 5½" strips.

4. Using the patterns on page 41, trace the small leaf and the large leaf onto template plastic and cut out on the line. Using a water-soluble marking pen, trace around the template on the right side of a green print scrap. Cut six small leaves and two large leaves, leaving a scant ¼" seam allowance all around.

ASSEMBLING THE QUILT TOP

1. Place the 9" stem along the center seam of the four-patch background, tucking the raw end into the ½" unsewn space, and pin in place. Stitch the opening closed. Place the remaining stems as shown in the diagram, tucking them under the center stem. Place the two shorter stems above the rim of the flowerpot; pin in place. Appliqué the stems, referring to the directions for "Appliqué" on page 75.

2. Position the leaves as shown and pin in place. Appliqué the leaves to the background. Place a small spot of glue on the back of each flower and place the flowers at the ends of the stems. Sew a button at the center of each flower.

3. Sew the 3¾" x 18½" blue-and-tan strips to the sides of the quilt top and press the seam allowances toward the border. Sew the 3¾" x 19" blue-and-tan strips to the top and bottom of the quilt top. Press toward the border.

FINISHING THE QUILT

1. Layer the quilt top, batting, and backing; baste the layers together as shown in "Putting the Quilt Together" on page 77.

2. Hand quilt a diagonal crosshatch pattern in the beige background blocks and a heart in the center of the basket. I quilted a wavy line in the borders.

3. Attach the binding to the quilt, referring to "Binding" on page 78.

4. See "Adding a Label" on page 79.

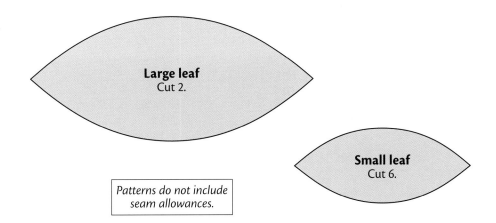

Large leaf
Cut 2.

Small leaf
Cut 6.

Patterns do not include seam allowances.

Summer 1861

July 1

Expected Mrs. Welch here to wash but [she] did not come so had the pleasure of doing it alone. Finished my new lawn dress and ironed some.

July 4

Waked up this morning by someone firing a gun near the house. Heard cannons at McHenry, Elgin, and Wauconda. Elias and Dexter made little cannons for their fourth. Clara had lots of little girls here and had a great time in their playhouse. I went to McHenry in the evening with John Simmons to the Gage House. Had a good party but never got supper until four o'clock in the morning.

July 8

Washed with a little of Anna's help. Had a dreadful storm. Wind did a great deal of damage in Rockford. Blowed my clothes all off the line and had to wash them all over again. Made some currant jelly. Got my work done and went to bed before sundown.

July 12

Mrs. Alcott and Dr. Benson here. Dr. said I was the first sensible girl he had seen because I had not cut my hair off.

July 13

Cleaned the kitchen floor, did some cooking, and after dinner Emma and I went to Mrs. Miller's to a quilting. All the women in the neighborhood went. Had one of the best times.

July 17

Mother, Aunty and all the rest of the women went to Mrs. Goodwin's to a quilting. Charley Patterson came here when they were gone. Em and I tried to tease him to join the Temperance Society. Could not get him to give his consent.

July 18

Worked like fun to get our work all done in the forenoon and all of the girls were invited to Mrs. Goodwin's to finish the quilt that was commenced yesterday. [Northern women were often busy making quilts for the soldiers.] Got it done and shook it over all the girls' heads. Em got a letter from Matt Butler at Alton. Mother got some cloth for street basques [stylish bodice] off a peddler and a new dress for herself.

July 23

Ironed all the forenoon and part of the afternoon before we got done. Emma, Anna, and I picked ten quarts of gooseberries — got our hands pretty well scratched up. Mr. Sargent came back about noon and told some very startling war news. [On July 21, 1861, the North suffered a defeat at the Battle of Bull Run, the first major conflict of the war.]

July 24

Washed the windows in the kitchen and pantry. While we were eating dinner, Mr. Smith came.

Quilting party, 1898

August 1

Did lots of work. Churned, made cheese, bread, pies, washed dishes, and [it was] very warm. Thermometer 95° in the afternoon and 91° at dinner. So warm we could not sew nor scarcely do anything else.

August 2

Hot, Hotter, Hottest. Enough to roast anybody.

August 4

Had breakfast at eight o'clock then got ready to go to meeting at half past ten. Very warm and the minister preached two hours and a half and then it was hard work for him to stop.

August 5

Cut the little girls some purple calico dresses.

August 7

Aunty sixty-eight years old today. Very warm. I took my sewing and ran away from the girls down in the woods then over to Mrs. Goodwin's and stayed until night and they did not know where I was.

August 8

Washed three calico dresses for myself and one for Em. Got dinner and after the work was done sewed on some embroidery. Finished the girls' dresses and cut out two night dresses for Mother and myself.

August 14

Alf Sellers and Josephine Patterson stayed all night. He was getting volunteers for the Woodstock Rifles. [The Woodstock Rifles was one of the first companies to enter into active service from McHenry County. It became Company H of the 36th Regiment, Illinois, Volunteer Infantry.] Myron promised to go and with Father's consent he stopped work and starts for camp on Tuesday.

August 18

Mother, Father, and the little girls went to Mrs. Marley's. She is quite sick on account of Henry's going to war.

August 19

Myron went to Woodstock to enlist. Felt a little bad to have him go and I guess he felt sorry to go. Augustus Patterson went and never came to bid any of us good-bye before going.

September 2

Did a very large washing so it would not be as large next week for I want to go to the fair. [The state fair was held in Chicago.] Monroe Shales and Adaline Moore married this morning. Fayette Robinson and Emma Butler stood up with them.

September 5

Came home from Mr. Vosburgh's and found Mr. Smith here. He has been very sick for two weeks. Was going home that night but I persuaded him to stay.

September 6

Mr. Smith and I played Euchre against Mother and Emma a little while. Then a visit to Mr. Miller's was proposed. Mother started first to tell them we were coming. Mr. Smith and I got there in time for dinner. Played Whist in the afternoon. About three o'clock Lester [Smith] and I came home and he bid [us] good-bye for he is to start next week for the war in a company of cavalry to be gone three years.

September 8

Emma and Sellers went to ride, then we bid Alf good-bye and he starts for the camp next Wednesday. James and Myron went to the station to Sabbath school — more to see the girls than anything else, I think.

September 11

Laura, Alice, Em, and I all went to Chicago to the State Fair. Us girls splurged round town that day and did not go to the fairgrounds on account of the mud. Went in the courthouse observatory and on Michigan Avenue. Felt pretty much tired out. Stayed with Alice at their cousin Mr. Andrus' on State St. Went to prayer meeting in the evening.

September 12

We all met in the morning and went to the Fair together. Found it very muddy. At noon, Father, Mother and I went to the Metropolitan Hotel and had dinner. Then did some shopping and came to the depot.

September 13

About all we did was to talk of the Fair and what we saw and did there. [Fairs in 1861 included the traditional livestock and agricultural exhibits, but also booths with handicrafts and sewing-machine demonstrations as well as handmade items for fundraising.]

September 19

Very warm in the afternoon. Was paring apples in the evening as busy as you please when Mr. Smith came very unexpectedly. He is home on furlough. Expects to start for Washington next week.

September 20

Rained all the forenoon the hardest I ever saw it in my life. Mr. Smith was in a great stew for he wanted to get home to attend some business. It slacked up so that he went home about three o'clock.

September 23

Aunty gave me a real scotch blessing [reprimand] — such a one as only she is capable of giving. It is rather unpleasant to have one member of the family always finding fault and watching so closely every crying thing unintentionally. Mother tells us not to mind her, for we must expect to put up with some things that are disagreeable to us.

September 26

Earl Thomas ran away last night to St. Charles to join the cavalry.

September 28

Emma sick all day and did not do much. I went to William's a little while in the evening. The rest played cards and I pieced calicos for my bed quilt.

September 30

Wanted to go to St. Charles to visit the boys in camp but guess we shall have to give it up, for we cannot get to the depot.

"We rode 38 miles on hard tires over dirt roads."

Photo was taken at Lake Marie, Illinois, in the late 1800s and includes Alice, Harry, and Hester Bennett (Adelia's children).

Orange Peel Quilt

This Orange Peel quilt contains a perfect blend of scraps and shirting prints. The border for the quilt was inspired by floral striped fabric seen in day dresses of the nineteenth century. Many of these types of fabrics eventually made their way into quilts.

FINISHED QUILT: 37" x 37"

FINISHED BLOCK: 6½" x 6½"

MATERIALS

Yardages are based on 42"-wide 100%-cotton fabrics.

¾ yard *total* of assorted scraps of light prints or shirtings for block backgrounds

⅝ yard of blue striped print for outer border (for crosswise stripe; ⅞ needed for lengthwise stripe)

¼ yard of brown print for inner border

Assorted scraps of medium to dark prints for block appliqué

⅜ yard of medium brown print for binding

1¼ yards of backing fabric

44" x 44" piece of cotton batting

Template plastic

CUTTING

From the scraps of light prints or shirtings, cut:
✦ 64 squares, 3¾" x 3¾"
✦ 4 squares, 4½" x 4½", from one print

From the brown print, cut:
✦ 2 strips, 1¾" x 26½"
✦ 2 strips, 1¾" x 29"

From the blue striped print, cut:
✦ 4 strips, 4½" x 29"

From the medium brown print, cut:
✦ 4 strips, 2½" x 42"

MAKING THE BLOCKS

1. Using the pattern on page 48, trace the appliqué shape onto template plastic and cut out on the line. With a water-soluble marking pen, trace the shape onto the right side of the assorted medium to dark print scraps. Cut out the shapes, adding a scant ¼" seam allowance all around. Cut 64.

2. Fold the 3¾" light print squares in half diagonally and finger-press. Place the appliqué shapes on the folded line right side up, leaving ¼" all around for seam allowances. Either hand baste or pin (using small appliqué pins) ¼" inside the drawn line. Finger-press the raw edge of the appliqué shape under to the drawn line. Choose a thread color that matches the print fabric. Starting on a straight edge and using your needle to help turn the finger-pressed shape, appliqué in place. (See "Appliqué" on page 75.) Make 64 units.

Make 64.

3. Sew four units together to make an Orange Peel block as shown. Press. Make 16 blocks.

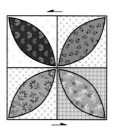

Make 16.

ASSEMBLING THE QUILT TOP

1. Lay out the blocks in four rows of four blocks each. Sew the blocks together into rows and press the seam allowances in opposite directions from row to row. Sew the rows together and press.

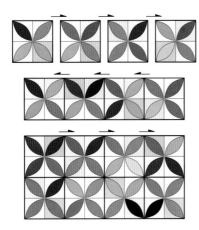

2. Sew the 1¾" x 26½" brown print strips to the sides of the quilt top and press the seam allowances toward the border. Sew the 1¾" x 29" brown print strips to the top and bottom of the quilt top. Press toward the border.

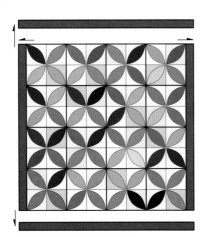

3. Sew two of the 4½" x 29" blue striped strips to the sides of the quilt top and press the seam allowances toward the outer border. Sew a 4½" light print square to each end of the remaining blue striped strips and press toward the borders. Sew these to the top and bottom of the quilt top and press toward the outer border.

FINISHING THE QUILT

1. Layer the quilt top, batting, and backing; baste the layers together as shown in "Putting the Quilt Together" on page 77.

2. This quilt was machine quilted with a stipple design.

3. Attach the binding to the quilt, referring to "Binding" on page 78.

4. See "Adding a Label" on page 79.

Orange peel
Cut 64.

*Pattern does not
include seam allowance.*

Charming Coins
Doll Quilt

Inspired by a photo of a coins charm quilt from the 1860s, this little quilt makes use of a variety of scraps. The saying goes that if you made a quilt from 1000 scraps, no two alike, your quilt would be "charmed"!

MATERIALS

Yardages are based on 42"-wide 100%-cotton fabrics.

¼ yard *total* of assorted scrap prints (each at least 1½" x 2½") for bars

¼ yard of light tan print for sashing

¼ yard of red print for side borders

¼ yard of medium green print for top and bottom borders

⅛ yard of green print for corner squares

¼ yard of dark blue print for binding

⅝ yard of backing fabric

22" x 27" piece of thin cotton batting

CUTTING

From the assorted scrap prints, cut:
✦ 72 rectangles, 1½" x 2½"

From the light tan print, cut:
✦ 3 strips, 2" x 18½"

From the red print, cut:
✦ 2 strips, 3" x 18½"

From the medium green print for borders, cut:
✦ 2 strips, 3" x 13"

From the green print for corner squares, cut:
✦ 4 squares, 3" x 3"

From the dark blue print, cut:
✦ 3 strips, 2" x 42"

ASSEMBLING THE QUILT TOP

1. Sew 18 of the 1½" x 2½" scrap rectangles together into a vertical row as shown. Make four vertical rows.

Make 4 rows.

2. Sew the light tan print strips and the pieced rows together as shown. Press the seam allowances toward the sashing strips.

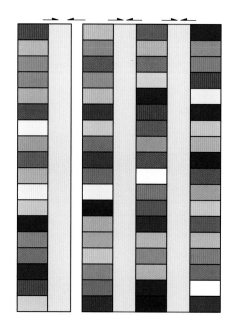

3. Sew the 3" x 18½" red print strips to the sides of the quilt top and press the seam allowances toward the border. Sew a 3" x 3" green square to each end of the 3" x 13" medium green strips and press toward the strip. Sew these to the top and bottom of the quilt top and press toward the border.

FINISHING THE QUILT

1. Layer the quilt top, batting, and backing; baste the layers together as shown in "Putting the Quilt Together" on page 77.

2. Quilt rows of Xs along the sashing strips. Stitch in the ditch along the rows of bars. Quilt diagonal lines in the borders and an hourglass in the corner blocks.

3. Attach the binding to the quilt, referring to "Binding" on page 78.

4. See "Adding a Label" on page 79.

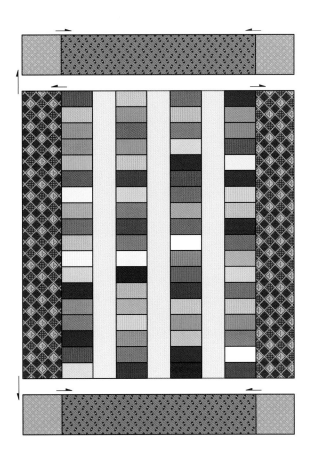

Civil War Baskets Quilt

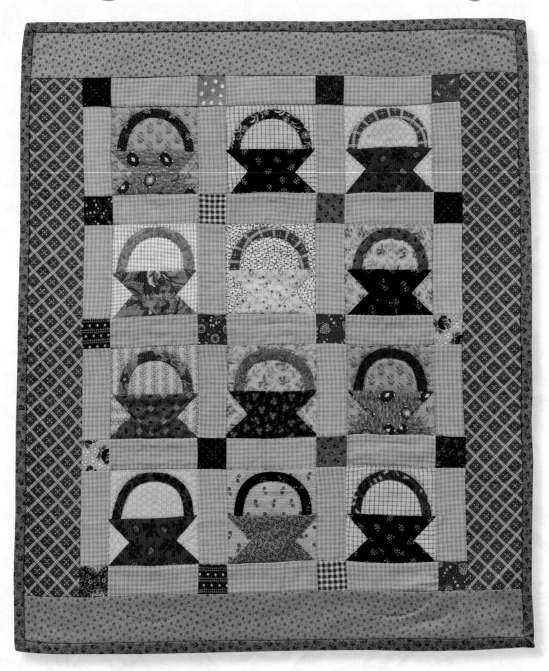

Women from the Civil War era often used baskets to hold their thread, buttons, scissors, scraps, or a small sewing project. Those of us who like to make scrap quilts today would need more than a few baskets to hold our scrap collections!

MATERIALS

Yardages are based on 42"-wide 100%-cotton fabrics.

½ yard *total* of assorted scraps of medium to dark prints for baskets and cornerstones

¼ yard *total* of assorted scraps of light tan prints for block backgrounds

¼ yard of blue checked fabric for sashing

¼ yard of brown print for side borders

¼ yard of gold print for top and bottom borders

¼ yard of bluish green print for binding

⅞ yard of backing fabric

26" x 31" piece of cotton batting

CUTTING

From the light tan prints, cut:

✦ 6 squares, 3¼" x 3¼"; cut each square *twice* diagonally to yield 24 quarter-square triangles

✦ 12 rectangles, 2½" x 4½"

From the assorted scraps of medium to dark prints, cut:

✦ 6 squares, 3¾" x 3¾"; cut each square once diagonally to yield 12 half-square triangles (you'll need 1 half-square triangle to match 2 quarter-square triangles cut below)

✦ 6 squares, 3¼" x 3¼"; cut each square *twice* diagonally to yield 24 quarter-square triangles

✦ 20 squares, 1¾" x 1¾"

✦ 12 bias strips, 1¼" x 6"

From the blue checked fabric, cut:

✦ 4 strips, 1¾" x 42"; crosscut into 31 pieces, 1¾" x 4½"

From the brown print, cut:

✦ 2 strips, 3" x 22¾"

From the gold print, cut:

✦ 2 strips, 2½" x 22½"

From the bluish green print, cut:

✦ 3 strips, 2½" x 42"

MAKING THE BLOCKS

Each Basket block consists of one light print for the background, one dark or medium print for the basket, and one contrasting bias strip for the handle. Select your fabrics before you piece each block.

1. To make the basket base, sew a medium print 3¼" quarter-square triangle to a light tan 3¼" quarter-square triangle. Press. Make 12 pairs.

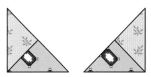

Make 12 pairs.

2. Sew the units from step 1 to the sides of a matching 3¾" half-square triangle. Press.

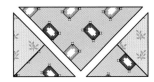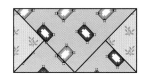

Make 12.

3. Referring to "Making Stems and Handles" on page 76, make a bias strip handle from a contrasting medium print and position it on a matching light tan 2½" x 4½" rectangle. Pin in place and stitch the handle to the rectangle. Make 12.

4. Sew each handle unit to a matching unit from step 2. Press. Make 12 blocks.

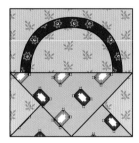

Make 12.

ASSEMBLING THE QUILT TOP

1. Sew three blocks together with four $1\frac{3}{4}$" x $4\frac{1}{2}$" blue checked sashing pieces to make a row. Press the seam allowances toward the sashing. Make four rows.

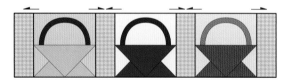

Make 4 rows.

2. Sew three $1\frac{3}{4}$" x $4\frac{1}{2}$" blue checked sashing pieces together with four $1\frac{3}{4}$" medium print squares to make a sashing row. Press toward the sashing. Make five sashing rows.

Make 5 rows.

3. Sew the block rows and the sashing rows together, pressing toward the sashing rows.

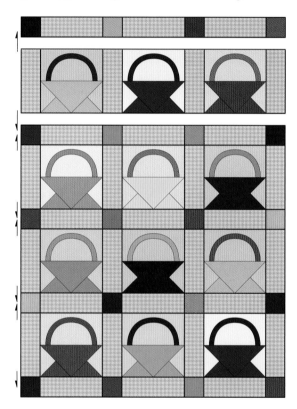

4. Sew the 3" x 22¾" brown strips to the sides of the quilt top and press the seam allowances toward the border. Sew the 2½" x 22½" gold strips to the top and bottom of the quilt top and press toward the border.

FINISHING THE QUILT

1. Layer the quilt top, batting, and backing; baste the layers together as shown in "Putting the Quilt Together" on page 77.

2. I hand quilted this quilt in the ditch along the baskets and quilted an X in the cornerstone squares. The border was quilted with a scalloped pattern using a bowl to trace the design.

3. Attach the binding to the quilt, referring to "Binding" on page 78.

4. See "Adding a Label" on page 79.

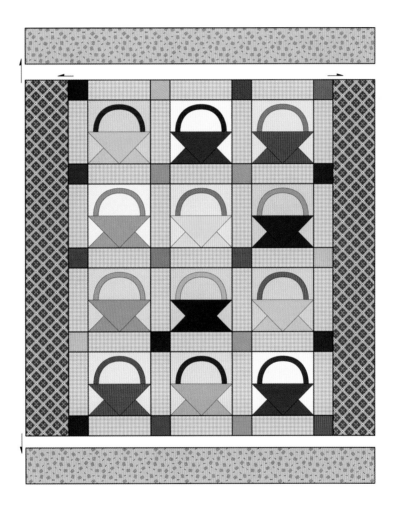

Fall 1861

Bennett family; Adelia in the center

October 1

Em and I went to visit Mrs. Town. Found Marg, Maria, Frank and Mrs. Jones, and Arvilla there to help Mrs. Town quilt, so we helped her also. Emma stayed all night and went with the rest of the girls to a surprise party [at] Mr. Butler's.

October 3

Mrs. Goodwin came over here for me to do some stitching on the machine. Mother and Father came home in the rain; bought a machine to pare apples with.

October 6

I went to Woodstock on my way to Rockford [to visit her Aunt Mary and Uncle Edwin]. After supper, Josephine and I went to Aunt Harriet's and went with her to hear Elder Lyon preach his favorite sermon. He starts tomorrow for St. Louis as Chaplain of the thirty-sixth regiment.

October 7

I went to Harvard to visit Miss Laura St. Clair. Walked between two and three miles and felt pretty well tired out when I got there. They were very glad to see me and I had a very good visit.

October 10

Amused myself playing on the piano, sewing, and most of all watching Aunt Mary work. I never saw anything beat it in all my life. If I had a sister ten years old that could not manage things better than she does, I should be ashamed of her.

October 12

Sewed most of the day and played with Herbert. Did not do much but visit. This is the day the Millerites [a religious movement of the time] prophesied that the world would come to an end. Didn't quite come to that time!

October 15

Did a little washing for myself and Aunt Mary in the morning and then helped her until noon. Took a little nap after dinner and then sewed the rest of the afternoon. Sewed and thought! Nothing to take my attention. No children, nothing to play with but a kitten and that too seems "old maidish," like its master and mistress.

October 23

This morning I went for Aunt Melinda to one of the neighbor's to buy some eggs. The wind blows today about as hard as yesterday. I finished the book I was reading and plaited [pleated] a dress skirt for Aunt Melinda that was Martha's. It was a very pretty dress and as I never plaited any before I had to fuss with it sometimes.

October 26

Josephine and I stayed [at] Aunt Ellen's until noon and went to Aunt Mary's to dinner. Went to a lecture on "the races" in the evening.

November 11

My little brother Eben who died nine years ago would have been eleven years old today. I went [to] town in the afternoon to get a paper for we were very anxious to hear the latest war news.

November 12

We just let all the work go in the forenoon and sewed on the machine. Called on my old friend and schoolmate, Susan Eddy, now Mrs. Sherman.

November 15

Sat with Mrs. Suiter in the afternoon and her little boy. Friend spilled ink all over her silk dress and himself too. Received a letter from Em saying that James had enlisted and wanted me to come right home.

November 17

Started for home about twelve o'clock. Arrived at four. Em had supper all ready. James had to go away in the evening a little while and as he was going back to camp early in the morning it left me with but little while to visit with him. He wanted me to sing so I sang one piece, "The Soldier Boy," which brought tears to his eyes [because] the words applied so good to him.

November 24

Charley Patterson came. Brought me a letter from Lester.

November 28

Thanksgiving day! Called in to William's to see Jule [for] the first time since he returned from the war sick. Made Elias a red flannel shirt and finished it that day and Clara a skirt in the evening. Emma cleaned the pantry. Very cold and snow on the ground. Emma went to sit up with the corpse of William Crabtree's little girl.

December 6

A man recruiting for Mulligan's Brigade in Chicago lectured at the schoolhouse and stayed here all night. Wesley Shepard and George Gill signed the muster roll.

December 7

The recruiting officer took the boys to Chicago today. Were all here for dinner. Elias went to the station and brought me a letter from Lester and one from Jim at St. Louis and a host of papers. Made Clara an apron today.

Bennett family in front of home, late 1800s;
Adelia on the far left, Chester on the far right

December 11

Mother went to Mrs. Goodwin's in the afternoon and left me to bake some brown bread. Had not been gone long before Melvira and Dave came. I forgot all about the bread and let it burn. Went after Mother and didn't she scold!

December 18

Mrs. Goodwin came here early in the morning to have me do some sewing for her on the machine and she put the facing on the girls' dresses for me. In the afternoon I went over to see how Jule was and to help Mrs. Vosburgh if she needed me. I swept, made some cookies, and did her ironing.

December 19

Mother made the stuff all ready for mince pies, chopped apples, and all that sort of thing getting ready for Christmas.

December 20

Mother made mince pies today, which took about all of her time. I made a housewife [sewing kit] for Lester, and Elias is going to Woodstock to carry it to be sent to Washington.

December 22

Got up this morning and the ground was white with snow. It continued to snow all day and it was about eight inches at night. Mr. Bennett was here and he was in a stew to know how he was going to get home. Anderson had to go home in the storm and break his own path. I think I never saw so much snow fall at one time.

December 23

Julius [Jule] Harback died today. He has been [sick] more than two months and is nothing but a skeleton.

December 25

Got up early and got the work done and the turkey in the oven and then went to Jule's funeral. Had a miserable sermon but a full house. He was buried in the Patterson place beside his mother. Found McComber's folks here when we got back. Got dinner as quick as we could. Edwin's folks, Uncle Johnson, Lydia, Jo, Em, and all hands here. Charley, Willie Thomas, Elias, Jo, and Em and myself went to Pingry's a little while. Bennett was one of the players.

December 26

Mother was called out in the night to Mrs. Stroop and did not get back until afternoon. [According to Civil War records, Mrs. Stroop's son was captured and imprisoned.] Last night received a photograph of four soldiers — Lester's and John Southworth and two strangers, no names attached.

[Adelia used blank pages at the end of the diary to continue her writing beyond the year and to add a detailed list of purchases she made in 1861.]

January 15, 1862

A large party came from McHenry — brought oysters and had supper. Asa W. Smith received a dispatch from Washington that Lester was very sick. Edwin told us of it.

January 20

Lester Smith died in the hospital at Alexandria, VA, of the typhoid fever.

January 28

His remains arrived at Woodstock (by express) to his brother, A.W. Smith, who the next day started for the East to bury him with his friends. [Lester Smith's obituary was found in the back of Adelia's diary.]

Adelia's 1861 Purchase List

.03	Steele thimble
1.25	Pair cloth boots
1.05	Black kid gloves
9.50	Cloak
3.75	Cotton cloth
3.75	1 doz. pairs of stockings
2.00	Preparation for hair
.60	Dressmaking
1.29	Hoop skirt
.20	Ruffle
1.00	Music
5.00	Shawl
1.33	Pressing hat, ribbon
1.75	Shoes
.66	Straps for trunk
3.62	Trunk
.98	Braid

Adelia's daughters, Grace, Alice, and Hester

Calico Comfort Nine Patch Quilt

Many women made quilts for family members going to war (if the men did not take family quilts with them). Quilts made specifically for the war were mostly utilitarian and often consisted of scraps sewn into a simple pattern, such as Nine Patch blocks.

MATERIALS

Yardages are based on 42"-wide 100%-cotton fabrics.

2 yards of black print for borders

1 yard *total* of assorted medium or dark print scraps for block centers

1 yard of blue print for setting triangles and corner triangles

¼ yard *total* of assorted light print or shirting scraps for block centers

28 strips, 2" x 20", of assorted medium and dark prints for blocks

22 strips, 2" x 20", of assorted light prints and shirtings for blocks

43 sets of 4 matching medium or dark print squares, 2" x 2", for blocks (172 total)

7 sets of 4 matching light print squares, 2" x 2", for blocks (28 total)

⅝ yard of brown print for binding

4½ yards of fabric for backing

71" x 81" piece of cotton batting

CUTTING

From *each* of the 22 light print strips, cut:

✦ 4 rectangles, 2" x 5" (88 rectangles total)

From *each* of the 28 medium or dark print strips, cut:

✦ 4 rectangles, 2" x 5" (112 rectangles total)

From the assorted light print scraps for block centers, cut:

✦ 10 squares, 5" x 5"

From the assorted medium or dark print scraps for block centers, cut:

✦ 40 squares, 5" x 5"

From the blue print, cut:

✦ 5 squares, 12" x 12"; cut each square *twice* diagonally to yield 20 setting triangles (2 will be extra)

✦ 2 squares, 6¼" x 6¼"; cut each square once diagonally to yield 4 corner triangles

From the black print, cut on the *lengthwise* grain:

✦ 4 strips, 5¼" x 72"

From the brown print, cut:

✦ 8 strips, 2½" x 42"

MAKING THE BLOCKS

For each block, lay out four matching 2" squares, four matching 2" x 5" rectangles, and one contrasting 5" square as shown. Sew the pieces into rows, pressing the seam allowances of the top and bottom rows toward the corner squares and the seams in the middle row toward the center square. Sew the rows together and press the seam allowances toward the center. Make 50 blocks.

Make 50.

ASSEMBLING THE QUILT TOP

1. Lay out the blocks and the blue print side and corner triangles in diagonal rows. Sew the blocks and side triangles together in rows, pressing the seam allowances in opposite directions from row to row.

2. Sew the rows together, matching seam intersections. Add the corner triangles and press toward the triangles.

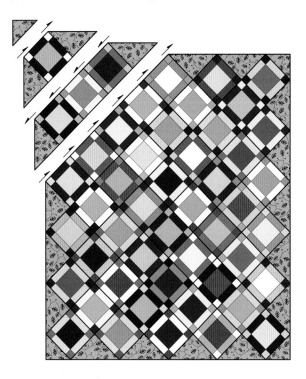

3. Trim the quilt top, leaving a ¼" seam allowance all around.

4. Measure the length of the quilt top through the center. Cut two of the 5¼" x 72" black print strips to fit and sew them to the sides of the quilt top. Press the seam allowances toward the border strips. Measure the width of the quilt top through the center, including the side borders just added. Cut the remaining 5¼" x 72" black print strips to fit and sew them to the top and bottom of the quilt top. Press toward the border strips.

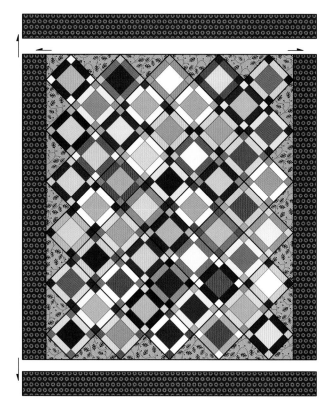

FINISHING THE QUILT

1. Layer the quilt top, batting, and backing; baste the layers together as shown in "Putting the Quilt Together" on page 77.

2. This quilt was machine quilted with an allover Baptist Fan design.

3. Attach the binding to the quilt, referring to "Binding" on page 78.

4. See "Adding a Label" on page 79.

Housewife Needle Case

Women of the eighteenth and nineteenth centuries stored their
sewing supplies in a small kit, called a **huswife** or **housewife**.
Soldiers enlisted in the Civil War did their own sewing and
uniform mending, so many of them also carried one in their
haversack to hold needles, thread, buttons, and perhaps scissors.
Many such needle cases were made by family members or loved
ones and given as sentimental tokens when men went off to war.

MATERIALS

Yardages are based on 42"-wide 100%-cotton fabrics.

5" x 12" scrap of reproduction print for case cover

5" x 12" scrap of reproduction print for case lining

Scraps of 3 contrasting prints for pockets, each at least 5" x 7½"

5" x 12" piece of thin cotton batting

3½" x 3½" square of felt

24"-long piece of grosgrain ribbon, ⅜" wide

1 button, ½" to ¾" in diameter

CUTTING

From *each* of the 3 contrasting prints for the pockets, cut:

✦ 1 rectangle, 5" x 7½" (3 total)

ASSEMBLING THE CASE

1. Fold the 5" x 7½" rectangles in half, wrong sides together, and press. Layer the rectangles on the right side of the lining, raw edges toward the bottom, beginning at the bottom and placing them 2" apart. Pin in place. Using a cup, lightly mark a line to round the corners on one end of the felt square and cut on the line. Center and pin the felt square 1½" from the top of the lining. Starting at the bottom, sew each pocket piece and the felt square to the lining, ¼"

from the raw edge, folding each one down after stitching so the piece isn't caught in the stitching above.

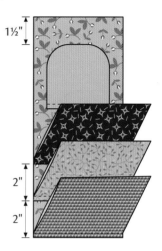

2. Layer the lining with the cover pieces right sides together. Place the 5" x 12" piece of batting on the bottom. Using a cup, lightly mark a curve at the top of the layered pieces. Cut on the line through all three layers to round the top corners. Using a scant ¼" seam allowance, sew the layers together, leaving a 2" opening for turning. Be careful to cover the stitching from the bottom pocket.

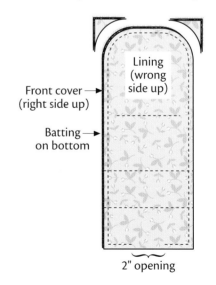

Front cover → (right side up)

Batting → on bottom

Lining (wrong side up)

2" opening

3. Turn the needle case right side out and press flat. Fold the seam allowances at the opening to the inside and sew completely around the case, ¼" from the edge.

4. Fold the case in thirds. Measure 8" from one end of the ribbon and mark that spot. Center the ribbon on the case and stitch in place about 1" from the rounded edge. Sew a button on top of the ribbon for a decorative effect.

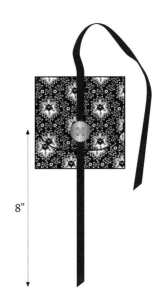

8"

Prairie Points Doll Quilt

Adelia lived on a farm in Illinois during the time she wrote her diary.
Illinois is also the Prairie State, so it seemed fitting to
include a quilt with Prairie Points.

MATERIALS

Yardages are based on 42"-wide 100%-cotton fabrics.

1 yard *total* of assorted light, medium, and dark print scraps for blocks and prairie points

½ yard *total* of 2 different light tan prints for setting pieces

½ yard of light blue print for borders

⅛ yard *total* of assorted medium blue print scraps for blocks

¼ yard of red print for binding

1 yard of backing fabric

28" x 34" piece of cotton batting

CUTTING

From the assorted light print scraps, cut:
✦ 48 rectangles, 1½" x 2½" (12 sets of 4 matching rectangles)

From the assorted medium print scraps, cut:
✦ 24 squares, 1½" x 1½"

From the assorted dark print scraps, cut:
✦ 24 squares, 1½" x 1½"

From the assorted medium and dark print scraps, cut:
✦ 38 squares, 3" x 3"

From the assorted medium blue print scraps, cut:
✦ 48 squares, 1½" x 1½"

From the 2 different light tan prints, cut:
✦ 6 squares, 4½" x 4½"
✦ 3 squares, 7" x 7"; cut each square *twice* diagonally to yield 12 setting triangles (2 will be extra)
✦ 2 squares, 3¾" x 3¾"; cut each square once diagonally to yield 4 corner triangles

From the light blue print, cut:
✦ 2 strips, 3¾" x 23"
✦ 2 strips, 3¾" x 24"

From the red print, cut:
✦ 3 strips, 2½" x 42"

MAKING THE BLOCKS

1. For each block, sew a 1½" medium print scrap square together with a 1½" dark scrap square. Press toward the dark fabric. Make two. Join two units to make a four-patch unit as shown. Make 12 four-patch units.

Make 12.

2. Sew two matching 1½" x 2½" light print rectangles to the sides of a four-patch unit. Press the seam allowances toward the four-patch unit. Sew a 1½" medium blue square to the short ends of two matching 1½" x 2½" light print rectangles. Press toward the blue fabric. Sew these to the top and bottom of the unit. Press toward the four-patch unit. Make 12 blocks.

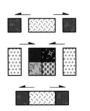

Make 12.

ASSEMBLING THE QUILT TOP

1. Lay out the blocks, the 4½" light tan print setting squares, and the light tan print side and corner setting triangles in diagonal rows. Sew the blocks, setting squares, and side triangles into rows, pressing the seam allowances toward the setting squares and triangles.

2. Sew the rows together, matching seam intersections. Add the light tan print corner triangles and press toward the triangles. If necessary, trim and square up the quilt top, making sure to leave ¼" beyond the points of all the blocks for seam allowances.

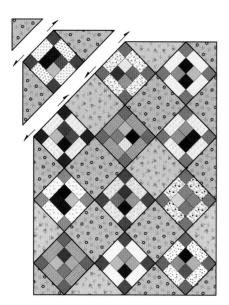

MAKING THE PRAIRIE POINTS

1. To make a prairie point, fold a 3" scrap square in half diagonally. Press. Fold the triangle in half diagonally again and press. Make 38 prairie points.

Make 38.

2. Place the prairie points evenly around the raw edge of the right side of the quilt as shown, tucking each one into the fold of the one next to it. Place 8 prairie points on the top, 8 on the bottom, and 11 along each side. Pin in place and machine baste the points a scant ¼" all around.

ADDING THE BORDERS

With the prairie points basted in place, sew the 3¾" x 23" light blue print strips to the sides of the quilt top. Press the seam allowances toward the border. Sew the 3¾" x 24" blue strips to the top and bottom of the quilt top and press toward the border. Give the prairie points an extra shot of steam to make them lie flat.

FINISHING THE QUILT

1. Layer the quilt top, batting, and backing; baste the layers together as shown in "Putting the Quilt Together" on page 77.

2. Quilt in the ditch around each block. I quilted a flower in the tan blocks, stitched an X in the Nine Patch blocks, and outlined the triangles.

3. Attach the binding to the quilt, referring to "Binding" on page 78.

4. See "Adding a Label" on page 79.

Turkey Tracks Quilt

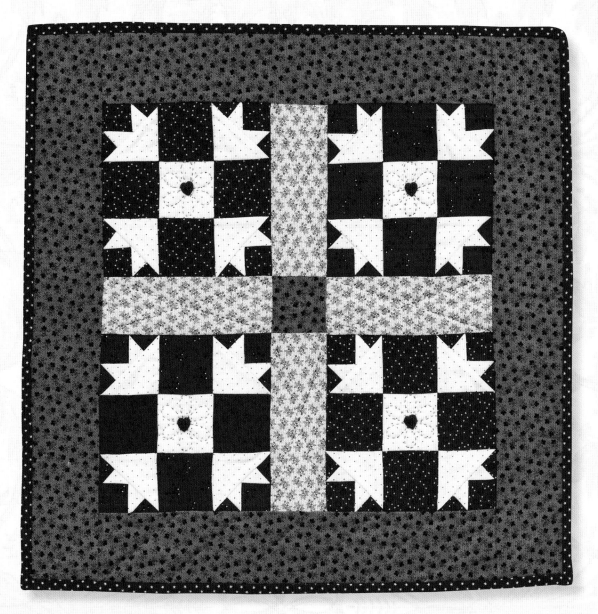

Turkey red and shades of green were popular colors used in quilts during the nineteenth century. The white dotted shirting prints also used in this quilt suggest winter snow, providing a nice contrast to the vivid colors used in the pattern.

MATERIALS

Yardages are based on 42"-wide 100%-cotton fabrics.

¼ yard of green print for borders and center square

⅛ yard *each* of 2 red prints for blocks

⅛ yard of white dotted fabric

⅛ yard of red-and-white print

¼ yard of red print for binding

¾ yard of backing fabric

23" x 23" piece of cotton batting

4 small heart-shaped buttons

CUTTING

From *each* of the red prints for blocks, cut:
- 8 squares, 2½" x 2½" (16 total)
- 4 squares, 2¼" x 2¼"; cut each square *twice* diagonally to yield 16 quarter-square triangles (32 total)
- 8 squares, 1½" x 1½" (16 total)

From the white dotted fabric, cut:
- 8 squares, 2⅞" x 2⅞"; cut each square *once* diagonally to yield 16 half-square triangles
- 8 squares, 2¼" x 2¼"; cut each square *twice* diagonally to yield 32 quarter-square triangles
- 4 squares, 2½" x 2½"

From the red-and-white print, cut:
- 4 rectangles, 2½" x 6½"

From the green print, cut:
- 1 square, 2½" x 2½"
- 2 strips, 3" x 14½"
- 2 strips, 3" x 19½"

From the red print for binding, cut:
- 3 strips, 2" x 42"

MAKING THE BLOCKS

1. For each block, sew a red quarter-square triangle to a white dotted quarter-square triangle, right sides together as shown. Press the seam allowances toward the red fabric. Make four and four reversed with matching red fabrics.

Make 4 of each.

2. Sew one triangle unit and one reversed triangle unit to adjoining sides of a matching 1½" red print square. Make four.

Make 4.

3. Sew a white dotted half-square triangle to the unit from step 2. Make four.

Make 4.

4. Lay out four matching units from step 3, four matching 2½" red print squares, and one 2½" white dotted square as shown. Sew the units together in rows. Press the seam allowances of the top and bottom rows toward the red

square. Press toward the red squares in the middle row. Sew the rows together. Press. Make two blocks from each of the red prints.

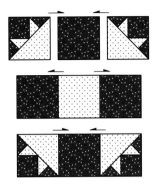 

Make 4.

ASSEMBLING THE QUILT TOP

1. Lay out the blocks, the four 2½" x 6½" red-and-white print rectangles, and the 2½" green print square in rows.

2. Sew the blocks, white print rectangles, and green print square into rows. Press the seam allowances in the top and bottom rows toward the rectangle. Press toward the rectangles in the middle row. Sew the rows together, and press.

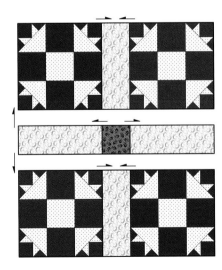

3. Sew the 3" x 14½" green print strips to the sides of the quilt top and press the seam allowances toward the border. Sew the 3" x 19½" strips to the top and bottom of the quilt top and press toward the borders.

FINISHING THE QUILT

1. Layer the quilt top, batting, and backing; baste the layers together as shown in "Putting the Quilt Together" on page 77.

2. Quilt in the ditch around each block and quilt an X in the sashing pieces. I quilted a flower in the center square of each Turkey Tracks block and outlined the square with a diamond shape. The border was quilted with diagonal lines spaced 1½" apart.

3. Attach the binding to the quilt, referring to "Binding" on page 78.

4. Add a small button to the center of each Turkey Tracks block.

5. See "Adding a Label" on page 79.

Grace Bennett, Elda Whitcomb Bennett,
Harry Bennett, Lucille Fitch,
and Alice Bennett (top)

Adelia's daughters, the Bennett sisters —
Grace, Alice, and Hester

Epilogue

Adelia Thomas was an average young woman of her time.

Like many young people today, social interactions and relationships with the opposite sex formed an important part of her life, as we can see from the journal pages. For many Northern women, far removed from the battlefields, the war did not become a reality until their lives were directly affected when the men in their homes and neighborhoods enlisted. In Adelia's case, I'm sure that the war became real as the year went on and she witnessed the deaths of those close to her and watched the impact the suffering of the war had on those around her. Many of the young men in her community enlisted, some of them close friends or family members. Several men died, several came home disabled, and some were captured and taken as prisoners of war.

For a young woman living in the nineteenth century, pressure to marry was high, and the war dashed many women's hopes. Adelia married Chester Bennett (Mr. Bennett) in January 1865 after a correspondence of several years. In one letter in particular written during their courtship, she complains to her future husband that these are "sorry times for the girls" in her town, with "nary a beau" to be found. Shortly after they were married, the couple moved to Tripoli, Iowa, where Mr. Bennett held a position as a schoolteacher. The war ended that year. President Lincoln was assassinated in April of 1865. The final death toll was over 600,000, and some historians claim it was as high as 700,000.

The couple eventually had a family, and a diary kept by her mother in 1877 notes visits from Adelia and the children. The Bennetts returned to Illinois in 1871, and settled in the town of Des Plaines. According to census records from 1880, Adelia and Chester had four children—Harry, 9; Hattie (or Hettie, short for Hester), 7; Alice, 3; and Grace, 1.

Adelia's brother Elias enlisted in the war at age 16, survived, and went on to have a family of his own. Adelia's three sisters—Emma, Clara, and Hettie—all died within 20 years after the diary was written. Adelia died on January 10, 1899, at the age of 57. Her grave in a Park Ridge, Illinois, cemetery has a marker with an emblem of the Women's Relief Corps, suggesting that she went on to become involved in volunteer work after the war. Chester Bennett died in 1916.

Women's lives changed considerably in the years after the war began. Northern women may not have been affected as severely as Southern women, primarily because the war was not fought on their soil. Yet their superb organizational skills gained through volunteer efforts in the war led to the formation of relief organizations like the Sanitary Commission, which made a huge contribution toward easing the suffering of Union soldiers during the war and also became the forerunner of the American Red Cross. It was these kinds of experiences, acquired through volunteering, that often led women into jobs after the war—jobs formerly only available to men. Thus, women's work that began during the Civil War is considered by some historians the impetus for the women's rights movement, which gained strength later in the century, and was certainly a turning point in the struggle for women's independence that forever changed the role of women in society and the workplace.

Quiltmaking Basics

Women of the nineteenth century did not have all the tools and techniques that are available to quilters today. Skills were passed down from generation to generation, and young women and even children were expected to help with sewing chores in the home. With the advent of the sewing machine in the middle of the century, those chores could be finished in one third of the time. Imagine how much more difficult quilting must have been for women then and how much time was taken away from their busy day. Yet the quilts that were made so long ago are often astonishing in their workmanship and design.

The quilts in this book use some of the traditional blocks that were popular in the nineteenth century. All that you need to make the quilts is a very basic sewing machine. Use a ¼" seam allowance and try to be accurate. If your machine does not have a ¼" foot, place a strip of masking tape on the throat plate exactly ¼" from the needle and use this as a guide as you are sewing.

BASIC TOOLS

Here's a list of tools to get you started.

Rotary cutter. A medium-sized cutter (45 mm) will enable you to cut strips and trim small pieces.

Rotary-cutting mat. Use this gridded surface for cutting fabric. An 18" x 24" mat is a good choice.

Ruler. Use a clear plastic ruler that is at least 4" x 12" and designed to be used with a rotary cutter. The measurements should also be clearly marked. A 6" square ruler also comes in handy.

Pins. Use sharp pins to hold your pieces while sewing. Small appliqué pins will keep small pieces from shifting.

Thread. Always use 100%-cotton thread for your piecing, and use quilting thread, which is coated, for hand quilting the top of your quilt.

Needles. Use 80/12 sewing-machine needles for machine piecing. Change your needle after every major project to be sure your needle is always sharp. You will need basic hand-sewing needles for sewing bindings, needles called Sharps for appliqué, and needles called Betweens for hand quilting.

Seam ripper. Expect to make some mistakes but don't worry too much about them. If you do make a mistake, a seam ripper can help you remove the stitches to correct it.

Iron and pressing surface. Any iron with a cotton setting will work for pressing your quilt pieces. You will need a flat surface for pressing, such as an ironing board or pressing mat.

ROTARY CUTTING

Accurate cutting is an important part of making any quilt, large or small. If your pieces are not cut properly, the piecing may be difficult and the quilt measurements will be off. Cutting is also important for conserving your fabric, although with many of these quilts, because they use a variety of scraps, more than enough yardage is given in the pattern directions.

While strip piecing and cutting doesn't generally work well with scrap quilts, as no two blocks are usually the same, you *can* layer your fabrics and cut multiple pieces at the same time.

PRESSING

Always press each seam after sewing. Press the seam allowances to one side, toward the darker fabric, if possible. When joining pieces, blocks, or rows of blocks, press the seam allowances in opposite directions to make lining up the seams (when sewing) less difficult. Pressing in this way will allow seams to line up more easily and the blocks will fit together nicely.

Opposing seams

SQUARING UP BLOCKS

Squaring up your blocks will ensure that the pieces of your quilt, the sashing, and the borders will fit together nicely. Before you piece your blocks together, check to see that they are the same size. Uneven blocks are usually caused by incorrectly sewing the seam allowances. Sometimes all that's needed is to redo a seam that is too little or too large. Also, check your pressing. Incorrect pressing can leave distortions in the pieces. If you use a steam iron, like I prefer to, make sure that you press carefully

without stretching the fabric or your pieces will definitely become distorted.

Find the center of your block and lay your clear, square ruler on top, using the grid lines to line up the pieces in the block and trim if they are uneven.

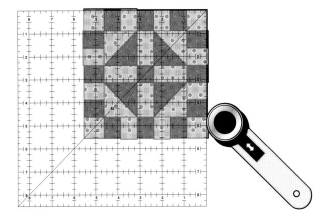

APPLIQUÉ

Some of the quilts in the book use simple needle-turn appliqué, which was the method used during the nineteenth century. When I first began quilting, I used to be afraid of the "A word" and steered away from any projects that included appliqué techniques, thinking that only very experienced quilters could master them. I still haven't quite mastered appliqué, but I'm no longer afraid to try, even if it means I still need to practice a bit and improve my skills along the way. So, even if you're an inexperienced quilter, try one of the appliqué projects in this book; if your first appliqué attempt isn't perfect, the next one will be better.

The needle-turn method of appliqué connects us to some of the methods quilters used in the nineteenth century and also lends a handmade rather than a polished look to the quilts. The appliqué designs in the book are relatively simple and the patterns few, providing an excellent way for you to try your hand at this technique without a lot of grief. If you practice enough (try the "Orange Peel Quilt" on page 46), your skills will improve.

The templates given do not include seam allowances. Trace around the shape onto a piece of template plastic and cut out. With a water-soluble marking pen or quilting pencil, trace around the shape on the right side of your fabric. Cut out the shape, leaving a scant ¼" seam allowance for turning under, and pin in place. Either hand baste or pin (using small appliqué pins) ¼" inside the drawn line. Finger-press the raw edge of the shape under to the drawn line. Choose a thread color that matches your fabric. Starting on a straight edge, and using your needle to help turn the finger-pressed shape, stitch in place with a blind stitch.

MAKING STEMS AND HANDLES

1. Cut the strips for stems and handles according to the project directions.

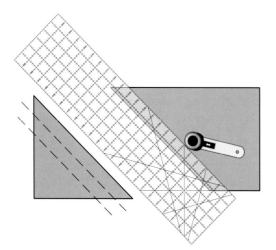

2. Fold the strips in half, wrong sides together, and press. Sew ¼" from the raw edge. Trim the seam allowance to ⅛".

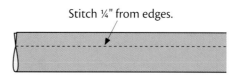

Stitch ¼" from edges.

3. Insert a pressing bar into the sewn strip or tube, turning the seam to the flat side of the bar so that it is hidden. Press the seam flat and remove the tube carefully (the pressing bars can get very hot).

Bias bar

4. Stitch in place with an appliqué stitch. For appliqué tubes that are curved, such as the basket handles on page 54, gently pull the handles to curve into the shape needed.

BORDERS

The border will do much to enhance the quilt if it's chosen well. Select the fabric for your quilt's borders after the quilt top is completed. Make sure the pattern isn't so busy that it detracts from the quilt. A good rule of thumb is, if the main part of the quilt is very busy with many scrappy pieces, try to tone it down with a "quiet" border, choosing fabric that has a low contrast instead of a large print. The border should frame the quilt, not take over. Lively borders work best when the rest of the quilt has a subdued tone and contains plain blocks or blocks with fewer contrasting pieces.

It's important to measure the sewn quilt top before cutting the border strips, especially on large quilts, since slight piecing variations can affect the measurements. Measure the center in both directions and cut the borders as directed.

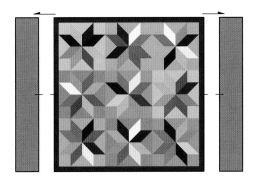

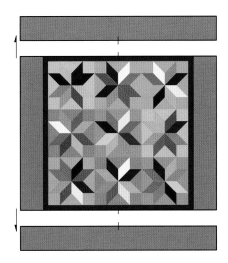

PUTTING THE QUILT TOGETHER

Square up the four corners of your quilt top using a square ruler. Trim the four sides, if necessary, by lining up your long ruler from one corner to the opposite corner and trimming away any excess fabric.

Some of the larger quilts in the book were made with pieced backings. Sew the pieces together with a ¼" seam allowance in one of

the three ways shown below. Cut the backing at least 3" larger in length *and* width than the quilt top.

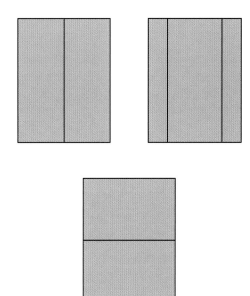

Use a thin, low-loft cotton batting for the soft, flat look seen in many antique quilts. Cut the batting at least 3" larger in length *and* width than the quilt top. Lay the backing on a clean, level surface. Smooth out any wrinkles and use masking tape to secure the corners. Layer the batting and quilt top over the backing. Baste or pin the layers together.

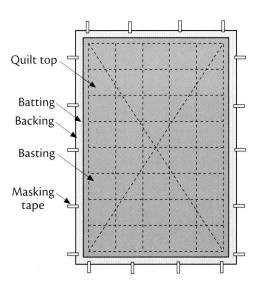

QUILTING

Quilts in the nineteenth century often featured simple quilting designs, and quilts made for utilitarian purposes featured the simplest designs of all, often straight-line quilting. Many of the small quilts in this book were quilted by hand and if you have the time, I highly recommend it for that antique look. Use a simple quilting design of your own or follow the examples in the quilts in the book.

Cut an 18" length of neutral-colored quilting thread (or one that matches the fabrics on the quilt top). Or, use a contrasting color of thread if you want your stitches to stand out. Try to keep your stitches even; however, sometimes a little irregularity in the stitches adds to the charm of the quilt. Remember, most antique quilts weren't perfect by any means, and part of their charm is in the handmade look.

BINDING

To bind your quilt, cut strips from binding fabric in the required width for your quilt. Measure around the quilt and add 10" extra for mitering corners and joining strips.

1. Join the strips using a diagonal seam and press the seam allowances open. Fold the strips in half, wrong sides together, and press.

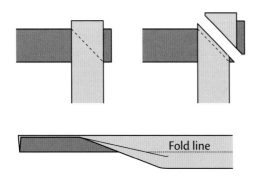

2. Using your ruler and rotary cutter, straighten the edges of the quilt and make sure the corners form right angles. Trim away excess batting and backing.

3. Position the binding along one side of the quilt top, aligning the raw edges.

4. Leaving a 5" piece of binding free, begin stitching the binding to the quilt top, starting at the center of one side and using a ¼" seam allowance. Sew through all three layers. Stop ¼" from the first corner and backstitch.

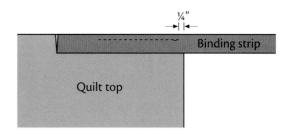

5. Remove the quilt from the machine. Turn the quilt and fold the binding straight up, making a 45° angle. Fold the binding back down, aligning it with the edge of the next side. Continue sewing the remaining sides in this way.

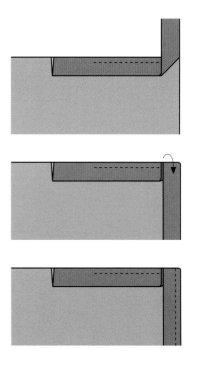

6. Stop stitching about 5" from the place you started and remove the quilt from the machine. Overlap the beginning and ending pieces of binding and trim so that the overlap equals the width that you cut your binding strips (2½").

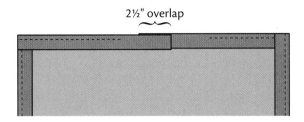

2½" overlap

7. Place the strips right sides together at a right angle. Sew on the diagonal and trim away the excess fabric. Lay the binding back over the quilt and finish sewing it in place.

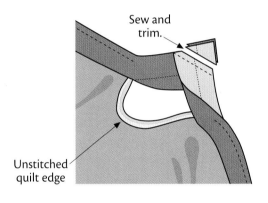

Sew and trim.

Unstitched quilt edge

8. Turn the binding over to the back of the quilt and stitch it to the quilt with a blind stitch using matching thread. Miter the corners as shown.

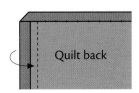 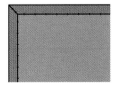

Quilt back

ADDING A LABEL

Many antique quilts survived without labels, but what a wonderful legacy it would have been if their makers had listed their names and dates or other information on the back. For a legacy of your own, add your name and date to the back of the quilt. Your family will thank you someday!

I like to make a simple label by ironing a piece of double-sided fusible web (for stability when writing) to a neutral piece of fabric or a small piece of muslin and then signing my name and date with a fine-tip permanent marker. Fuse the label to the back of the quilt. Hand stitch ⅛" along the edge with a simple running stitch in a contrasting-colored thread, picking up the fabric of the backing and making sure you don't stitch through to the front of the quilt.

Kathleen Tracy
2008

References

Howard, Robert P. *Illinois: A History of the Prairie State.* Grand Rapids, MI: Wm E. Erdman Publishing Co., 1972.

Kiracofe, Roderick. *The American Quilt: A History of Cloth and Comfort 1750–1950.* New York: Clarkson Potter, 1993.

Leonard, Elizabeth D. *Yankee Women.* New York: W.W. Norton & Co., 1994.

Moore, Frank. *Women of the War: True Stories of Brave Women in the Civil War.* New York: Blue/Grey Books, 1997.

Silber, Nina. *Daughters of the Union: Northern Women Fight the Civil War.* Cambridge, MA: Harvard University Press, 2005.

About the Author

Kathleen Tracy made her first small quilt from a Martingale & Company pattern book she picked up in 2000. Making quilts for her daughter's American Girl dolls sparked an interest in history and led to the publication of *American Doll Quilts* (Martingale & Company) in 2004. Kathleen looks to antique quilts for inspiration in making her scrappy quilts from simple blocks; she hopes that her books make the past come alive and give quilters a connection with quilters from long ago. She is also the author of *Prairie Children and Their Quilts* (Martingale & Company, 2006). Kathleen is a frequent lecturer to quilt guilds across the country and conducts workshops on making small quilts with an antique look.

In addition to quilting, Kathleen is an avid reader and loves gardening, cooking, and making simple beaded jewelry for family and friends. She lives in Deerfield, Illinois, with her husband, college-aged son, teenage daughter, and their two dogs. Kathleen loves to hear from other quilters and welcomes comments. Visit her at www.countrylane quilts.com.